An Illustrated Brief History of
CHINESE GARDENS

An Illustrated Brief History of
CHINESE GARDENS
People | Activities | Culture

by Alison Hardie

SCPG

Copyright © 2023 Shanghai Press and Publishing Development Co., Ltd.

Text: Alison Hardie

Cover Design: Wang Wei
Interior Design: Li Jing (Yuan Yinchang Design Studio)

Editor: Wu Yuezhou

ISBN: 978-1-93836-887-5

Address any comments about *An Illustrated Brief History of Chinese Gardens* to:

SCPG
401 Broadway, Ste. 1000
New York, NY 10013
USA

or

Shanghai Press and Publishing Development Co., Ltd.
Floor 5, No. 390 Fuzhou Road, Shanghai, China (200001)
Email: sppdbook@163.com

Printed in China by Shanghai Donnelley Printing Co., Ltd.

1   3   5   7   9   10   8   6   4   2

Quanjing provides the images on pages 14, 40 (below) and 131 (above). CFP provides the images on the front cover (above) and pages 2–3, 10, 11 (above), 12, 21, 22, 31 (above), 32, 34–36, 40 (above), 44, 48 (below), 54 (below), 55, 68 (above), 70, 71 (above), 76, 83, 88, 92, 93 (below), 110, 111 (above), 112 (below), 115 (below), 121, 126 (below), 130, 133 (above), 134 (above), 138, 140 (below), 145, 148, 150 (right), 151, 152, 155 (below).

On page 1

Fig. 1   Please refer to fig. 144 on page 120.

On pages 2–3

Fig. 2   The so-called Summer Palace to the north-west of Beijing. In the mid-18th century, the park was named the Garden of Clear Ripples. It was renamed Garden for Maintaining Harmony (*Yihe yuan*) after reconstruction at the end of the 19th century.

Above

Fig. 3   Detail of *The Garden of Solitary Enjoyment*. Please refer to fig. 51 on pages 46 and 47.

Facing page

Fig. 4   Please refer to fig. 60 on page 53.

CONTENTS

Above
Figs. 5 and 6   Please refer to fig. 28 on page 27.

Figs. 7 and 8 *Elegant Gathering in the Apricot Garden* (detail)

Anon. (15th century), after Xie Huan (1346–1430)
Ink and color on silk
Dimensions of the complete handscroll: height 37.1 cm, length 243.2 cm
Metropolitan Museum of Art, New York

This handscroll painting records a gathering of scholar-officials that took place in Beijing in 1437. Gardens provided the setting for networking among social groups, whether scholar-officials (as here), merchants, or educated women.

INTRODUCTION

There are many books published in English on Chinese gardens, but the majority are primarily picture books with little informative content. Maggie Keswick's *The Chinese Garden: History, Art, and Architecture*, first published in 1978 and reprinted several times since, remains the standard introduction to the subject. Since 1978, however, scholarly research on Chinese gardens and landscapes has increased enormously and has been extended from the esthetic focus which was Keswick's primary interest to take in many other aspects, particularly the social function of gardens (figs. 7 and 8).

It is more than time for a new introduction to Chinese gardens which takes account of the research undertaken in recent decades and which is accessible to the general reader—who may be interested in garden history, or perhaps planning a trip to China—and to students taking courses in Chinese culture, whose numbers have increased beyond anything that could have been imagined in the late 1970s.

Since my own interest lies in the social uses of Chinese gardens and landscapes, that is the approach which I am employing to structure the present book, which I hope will be useful to the types of readers I have indicated.

I would like to thank all those who have helped me to learn about Chinese gardens over the years, especially Zhong Ming, to whose memory this book is dedicated.

The Development of Chinese Gardens

The book starts by outlining what little we know about gardens and parks in ancient China, up to the Han dynasty (206 BC–AD 220). The second chapter covers the period between the fall of the Han and the reunification of China under the Sui dynasty (581–618), and then the three centuries of the Tang dynasty (618–907), an era of great cultural splendor (fig. 9).

Fig. 9 *Honored Consort Yang Teaching a Parrot to Recite Buddhist Scriptures*
Mural painting from Liao dynasty tomb (916–1125), Baoshan, Inner Mongolia Autonomous Region

Honored Consort Yang (719–756) was the favorite consort of the Tang Emperor Xuanzong (685–762), whose reign in the 8th century was remembered as the cultural high point of the Tang dynasty. Here she is shown with attendants and her pet parrot in the palace garden, indicated by the bamboo on the left of the image.

The Tang forms a turning point from the grand imperial and aristocratic landscape parks and gardens of that early period, to an esthetic appropriate to the more modest circumstances of the growing class of literati whose official careers depended on their intellectual ability more than on the advantages of birth. This esthetic became entrenched during the succeeding Song dynasty (960–1279), when China's form of government changed decisively from an aristocratic to a bureaucratic system which was, nominally at least, a meritocracy (fig. 10).

The gardens of the Yuan dynasty (1279–1368) which came between the Song and the late imperial period of the Ming (1368–1644) and Qing (1644–1911) have been little studied, but despite the short duration of the dynasty—less than one hundred years—it was probably crucial in consolidating the idea of the garden as a hermit's retreat, a concept which played an important role in garden culture in the succeeding dynasties.

The Ming and Qing are the dynasties for which we have the most abundant information on gardens, and the so-called "scholar gardens" of this period, the gardens of the literati, especially those of the Ming, are regarded as the "classical" form (fig. 11). But the apparent dominance of the literati garden should not blind us to the existence of other types of garden, or indeed to the use of literati gardens by others who were not literati. In this section of the book I will discuss the involvement in garden culture of merchants, women, and craftsmen, as well as that of the literati and members of the imperial family whose gardens are generally celebrated.

At the beginning of the 20th century, China's Republican revolution meant that the society which had underpinned the existence of "scholar gardens" and other types of traditional garden came to a permanent end, but a fascination with "the Chinese garden" remains, and it has become a symbol of wider Chinese culture (fig. 12).

As this book is intended as a *social* history

Fig. 10 View of the Canglang Pavilion garden, Suzhou, Jiangsu Province

This Suzhou garden is famous as the site acquired by the Song-dynasty scholar-official Su Shunqin (1008–1048) after his dismissal from office for alleged corruption. Here he built a pavilion which he named Canglang in reference to a traditional rhyme exhorting officials to adapt to the circumstances of their time. The garden as it can be seen today is a much later creation.

of Chinese gardens, I focus on how gardens have functioned and been used in Chinese society through the ages. There are already many introductions to the esthetics of Chinese gardens available in English, ranging from the academic to popular coffee-table books. Readers who wish to understand more about the esthetic, philosophical, or other aspects of Chinese gardens will find suggestions for background reading at the end of this book, where there are also suggestions for those who would like to know more about the research (mostly recent) on which the individual chapters here are based. I strongly recommend that anyone reading this book should first look at images of Chinese gardens, in books or online, and preferably read a basic general introduction to the topic, so that they have in mind a rough idea of what Chinese gardens look like and why they include the elements which they do.

In this introduction, I will briefly consider the interplay between gardens, landscapes, and society, particularly within the framework of Chinese culture but also more widely. It is only by looking at the bigger picture that we can see what is special about the social role of Chinese gardens and landscapes in particular.

Fig. 11 The Garden of the Artless Administrator (*Zhuozheng yuan*) in Suzhou, Jiangsu Province, often known as the Humble Administrator's Garden or Garden of the Unsuccessful Politician, is frequently cited as an example of a Ming-dynasty scholar garden. In fact, although the present garden retains elements of the original 16th-century layout, it is almost entirely a modern reconstruction.

Fig. 12 The Garden of Flowing Fragrance (*Liufang yuan*), Huntington Botanical Gardens, San Marino, California

The Chinese garden in the Huntington Botanical Gardens, first created in the 1990s, is an adaptation of classical Chinese garden style to the climatic and geological conditions of California. Its development and expansion has been strongly supported by the large East Asian community in the Los Angeles area. (photo by author)

Differences and Similarities between Gardens in the East and West

When we use the English words "garden," "park," and "landscape," we think of these as different types of spatial construct. A garden may be quite small, and may be used to grow fruit and vegetables as well as flowers. A park may be attached to a large country house, or it may be a public green space in a town or city. A landscape may be wild and remote, perhaps defined as an area for nature conservation, or it may refer to a more "domesticated" agricultural landscape. Of course, all these different types of spatial construct also have their social aspects. What kind of people own, use, or are employed in them? Is access controlled, and if so, how? In what ways do the design and use of gardens reflect wider social issues? These are the types of questions which the social history of gardens attempts to answer.

How, if at all, do the concepts behind the English words "garden,""park," and "landscape" match similar concepts in Chinese language and culture? In modern Chinese, the basic term for a garden is *yuan* 园, but a distinction is made between *huayuan* 花园 (literally "flower garden"), which is closely equivalent to the English word "garden" meaning a fairly small, mainly decorative garden attached to a house, and would often be understood as a Western-style rather than Chinese-style garden, and *yuanlin* 园林 (literally "garden grove"), which is generally used to refer to a garden, whether large or small, in a traditional Chinese style. When talking or writing about "Chinese gardens" in general, it would be normal to use the expression *zhongguo yuanlin* 中国园林 (literally "Chinese garden groves"). A garden-like enclosure used primarily for the practical purpose of producing fruit or vegetables may be called *pu* 圃 —meaning "orchard" or

Fig. 13   Taoranting Park, Beijing
This public park in the southern part of central Beijing was established in 1952. It combines a generally Western-style layout with some Chinese-style buildings and other elements.

"(vegetable) plot"—or *yuanpu* 园圃—"garden plot."

As far as "parks" are concerned, modern Chinese makes a clear distinction between public parks—which in their modern sense were introduced to China only in the second half of the 19th century—and the type of park historically associated with imperial or aristocratic estates. Public parks (fig. 13) are *gongyuan* 公园 (literally "public garden"), while the basic term for large estates is *yuan* 苑 (pronounced with a different tone, *yuàn*, from *yuán* meaning garden), which implies a large enclosed space. The word is defined in *Hanyu Da Cidian*, the standard dictionary of Chinese, as "the old name for a place where birds and beasts are raised and trees are cultivated, usually referring to the garden groves of emperors, princes, and nobles."

The addition of the word *you* 囿 , an ancient word which has various meanings including an imperial or royal park (similar to *yuàn*), a vegetable garden or orchard, and more generally a defined piece of territory, gives the term *yuànyòu* 苑囿, defined as "a garden grove for raising birds and beasts for the enjoyment of emperors and princes in ancient times." Given that modern Chinese words tend to be disyllabic while ancient Chinese mainly used monosyllables, the term *yuanyou* is simply the modern equivalent of the traditional *yuàn*.

The English word "landscape" has a number of equivalents in modern Chinese. Perhaps the most widely used is *shanshui* 山水, which literally means "mountain and water." This is the term always used to refer to "landscape painting" (*shanshui hua* 山水画), and often to actual landscapes (fig. 14). However, a landscape in the sense of a scenic view can be called *fengjing* 风景, which also means "scenery," and *fengjing yuanlin* 风景园林 ("scenery garden") is often

Fig. 14 *Landscape Responding to the Art Theories of Wang Shizhen*

Huang Binhong (1865–1955)
Hanging scroll, ink and color on paper
Height 105 cm, width 43.2 cm
Tianjin Museum

This vertical hanging scroll by the great painter Huang Binhong is a modern example of traditional landscape painting, a genre which also includes paintings of gardens. The artist's inscription on this painting indicates that he was influenced not only by the Tang painter-poet Wang Wei (see fig. 44 on page 39), but also by the Ming writer and critic Wang Shizhen (see fig. 95 on page 81), who wrote on art as well as literature.

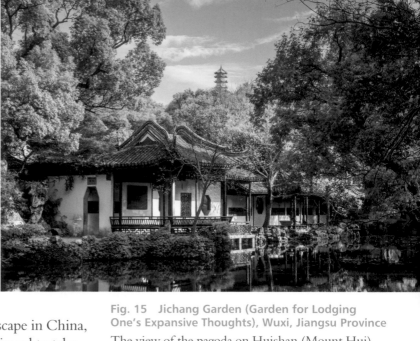

used as the equivalent of the English term "landscape garden." Another term for landscape is *jingguan* 景观, which literally means "scenic view." *Fengjing* and *jingguan* seem to emphasize the esthetic aspect of landscape, while *shanshui* incorporates both the esthetic and the physical.

Although a landscape is usually something much more extensive than a garden, gardens are intimately connected with landscape in China, because gardens were often designed to take advantage of views of the wider landscape, so-called "borrowed views" (*jiejing*; fig. 15), and also because gardens and features within them were often conceptualized as miniatures of greater landscapes or landscape elements such as mountains or lakes. Particular landscapes could also be treated almost like gardens, for example by constructing pavilions at specific viewpoints or adding inscriptions to call attention to some aspect of the scene or its historical associations (fig. 16). One cannot, therefore, consider either gardens or landscapes in isolation from each other.

Fig. 15 Jichang Garden (Garden for Lodging One's Expansive Thoughts), Wuxi, Jiangsu Province
The view of the pagoda on Huishan (Mount Hui) from the garden is one of the most famous borrowed views in traditional Chinese gardens. This garden inspired an imitation in one of the imperial gardens of the Qing dynasty.

Development of Chinese Garden Studies

Generally speaking, then, we can see that the English and Chinese terms for "garden," "park," and "landscape" are roughly equivalent to each other. We should note here that these are modern Chinese terms (though some were used in pre-modern times also) and have been influenced by the use of similar or equivalent terms in English or other European languages as Chinese intellectuals began to adopt modern "scientific" concepts and terminology from beyond

Fig. 16 Inscriptions on Seven Stars Cliff, Zhaoqing, Guangdong Province.

China's borders, particularly from the early 20th century onwards. In fact, the study of Chinese garden and landscape history within China has been significantly influenced by academic concepts originating in the West and often mediated through Japan, where two influential Chinese scholars of garden history, Liu Dunzhen (1897–1968) and Chen Zhi (1899–1989), studied in the first half of the 20th century. Others, such as Tong Jun (Tung Chuin, 1900–1983), studied in the United States.

In China, most of the scholars who have specialized in garden history have come from a background of architectural training, and since the early 20th century, garden design has been conceptualized as a branch of architecture. Much of the early research on Chinese garden history was carried out by members of the Association for Research in Chinese Architecture (*Zhongguo yingzao xueshe*) (fig. 17). It was perhaps their architectural training which influenced these scholars in focusing their research primarily on formal and esthetic aspects of gardens, a focus which continued until at least the 1980s. In the West, by contrast, although landscape studies are usually linked with architecture, in the case of the study of Chinese gardens many scholars have come from a background in art history. This has given them rather a different focus: as a result of the rejection of the classic esthetic approach in Western art history, and an increasing interest from the second half of the 20th century in the social history of art and art-works, Western scholars have perhaps been less willing to take on trust what owners of gardens in the past claimed for them as spaces protected from the pressures of official life and providing a place of pure reclusion. Very few scholars in China or the West now would take such claims at face value. Instead the gardens can be seen as actively promoting the owner's self-image and interests within society. As the Scottish landscape artist Ian Hamilton Finlay observed, "Certain gardens are described as retreats when they are really attacks."

This focus on the social history of gardens and landscapes has helped to develop a much more nuanced understanding of "the Chinese garden," moving us away from essentialized ideas of Chinese gardens as somehow unchanging and detached from the everyday world. A realization of the ways in which Chinese gardens were inextricably linked with the wider society makes them, in fact, much more interesting. As we explore these links, we can gain a deeper understanding not only of Chinese gardens but of Chinese society and culture as a whole. We can see how gardens functioned as real estate, how they gave opportunities of employment to skilled craftsmen, how they opened up outdoor space to both elite and lower-class women, how they allowed men of different social classes and of different ethnicities to interact and gain mutual benefit: in short, how the existence of gardens exerted an influence on society as a whole. At the same time, we can see how the wider society, and even socio-economic changes beyond China's own borders, had an impact on how gardens in China developed.

Fig. 17 In 1930 Zhu Qiqian (1872–1964) founded the Association for Research in Chinese Architecture. He was inspired by his responsibility, as a Beijing government official, for maintenance of the imperial palace buildings after the departure of the "last emperor." Zhu realized that traditional construction and craft skills would be lost unless they were studied and recorded.

PART I

GARDENS FROM EARLIEST TIMES TO THE 14TH CENTURY

This first section introduces the origins of the Chinese garden tradition, outlining the little we know of gardens in pre-imperial times, and then moving on to the imperial period from the Qin dynasty (221–206 BC) onwards. Information on gardens in the Han dynasty is largely confined to imperial gardens, while in the following period of disunion, between the end of the Han and the reunification of China under the Sui, we see the earliest beginnings of a distinctive culture of literati or scholar gardens. At the same time the literary origins of many later traditions are established, for example in the poetry of the archetypal "recluse" Tao Qian (Tao Yuanming, 365–427). After the short-lived Sui dynasty had reunified the empire and been succeeded by the long-lasting Tang dynasty, garden culture reached great heights of splendor, with magnificent imperial parks and gardens, and smaller but still impressive gardens created by the growing numbers of scholar-officials who had gained government office through the newly expanded route of competitive examinations. This laid the foundations for the cultural dominance of literati gardens in later times.

After the collapse of the Tang and its eventual replacement by the Song dynasty, the power of the aristocracy gave way decisively to the bureaucratic system under which China was governed for the remainder of the imperial period; this in turn influenced the way that garden culture developed. Although imperial gardens remained very important, and to some extent publicly accessible, during the Song dynasty, private gardens became a means for the now dominant scholar-official class to assert their cultural superiority. When the northern half of China was conquered by the Jin dynasty (1115–1234), established by the Jurchen, a non-Han ethnic group from the north-east, the Southern Song (1127–1279) established their capital in the gentle and fertile landscape of Hangzhou, introducing new ideals of what a landscape garden should resemble.

When China was once again unified under the alien government of the Mongol Yuan dynasty, most educated Han Chinese either voluntarily or forcibly abandoned government service. Again, this social change had far-reaching effects on garden culture, increasing the emphasis on the garden as a retreat from society and a hermit's sanctuary, an attitude which remained important even in the different social conditions of the following Ming and Qing dynasties.

Fig. 18   Please refer to fig. 44 on page 39.

CHAPTER ONE
EMPERORS AND ARISTOCRATS
FROM ZHOU TO HAN

In this early period, parks which were the preserve of emperors were used for hunting and for the production of food and other resources, as well as for seeking contact with supernatural powers, displaying the secular power of the monarch, and providing the ruling family with a pleasant living environment. People at the highest levels of society probably imitated imperial parks on a smaller scale, while gardens belonging to commoners were used primarily for the production of fruit and vegetables and of other plant-based materials. There is very little evidence of gardens at lower social levels being used for leisure rather than practical purposes, partly because people at these levels had very little leisure in any case. However, the cultivation of parks and gardens in the Han dynasty laid the foundations for the much greater development of garden culture in the period following the end of the Han.

Gardens in Poetry

Gardens of some sort have probably existed since the earliest development of settled agriculture in China, but despite China's long history of written records very little is known about early gardens. Archeological excavations are now starting to reveal some information from very early times. For example, excavation of an early Shang (2nd millennium BC) walled site at Yanshi in Henan Province revealed the existence of a long, narrow pond in the northern part of a walled palace area. The rectangular, man-made pond was connected to the palace moat through an inflow and a covered drainage ditch, thus ensuring the circulation of water; this shows the sophistication of hydraulic engineering in this early period.

The little that can be gleaned about gardens from the early period of literacy, in the *Book of Songs* (or *Book of Odes*, *Shijing*), a collection of about three hundred poems probably dating from the 12th to the 7th century BC, suggests that gardens were primarily used as productive spaces. One poem speaks of a garden containing peach and jujube (Chinese date) trees, another of a fenced garden with willows. In another—evidently a folk-song—a young woman begs her lover: "Do not climb into our homestead, Do not break the willows we have planted … Do not climb over our wall, Do not break the mulberry-trees we have planted … Do not climb into our garden, Do not break the hard-wood we have planted."[1] In each verse, she explains that she does not care about the plants, but about what her family and neighbors might say about her behavior!

The *Book of Songs* contains a number of what are evidently hymns or chants, presumably to be sung on ritual occasions. One of them describes the construction by the semi-legendary King Wen of Zhou (11th century BC?) of the Numinous Terrace

Fig. 19 Bronze vessel with hunting scenes
Warring States period
Diameter 26 cm, height 41.4 cm
Chengdu Museum

On this elaborately decorated bronze vase, the band of decoration between the handles shows a hunting scene, including a man spearing a leopard and another man shooting an arrow at a running stag.

Gardens of Zhou Rulers

It is likely that the rulers of the various states which constituted early China in the Spring and Autumn (770–476 BC) and Warring States (475–221 BC) periods followed King Wen in having parks of this kind, which were not just productive (of game, timber, and probably fruit) but also both esthetic and symbolic of the ruler's power. The construction of terraces like King Wen's Numinous Terrace was certainly undertaken by many Zhou rulers not only for viewing the wider landscape but also, perhaps primarily, to bring them closer to heaven, for the purpose of observing natural and astronomical phenomena and making contact with spirits and deities. An example of one of these terraces is the Gusu Terrace of King Fuchai (reigned 495–473 BC) of the state of Wu. However, historical records relate that in the associated pond or lake he enjoyed himself on a "dragon boat" with the beautiful Xi Shi, accompanied by performers playing music: this description suggests that the leisure and entertainment function of the park was starting to overtake the productive or religious function.

(*Lingtai*) in his Numinous Park (*Lingyou*), where there were deer, white herons, and fish in a Numinous Pool (*Lingchi*). This indicates that early rulers had parks where wild animals were preserved for hunting (fig. 19). It appears that the meat for which they were hunted was not just for royal, human consumption but also—perhaps primarily—for sacrifice to the gods. The use of the term "numinous" indicates that this park was conceived as a sacred space as well as a practical one.

Both the *Book of Songs* and another early collection of poems, the *Songs of the South* or *Songs of Chu* (*Chuci*), some of which may date from the 4th century BC, refer to many different kinds of plants, often using various flowers and weeds as metaphors for good or bad moral qualities. However, it is seldom clear, especially in the *Songs of the South*, whether these plants are growing wild or in some form of garden enclosure.

Two of the poems in the *Songs of the South* are shamanistic chants, probably from the 3rd century BC, to summon back the soul of a sick king or prince, by describing the terrors of the regions in which his soul might wander and the delights of the home to which he should return, where:

> Streams and gullies wind in and out,
>   purling prettily;
> A warm breeze bends the melilotus
>   and sets the tall orchids swaying …
> Seated in the hall, leaning on its
>   balustrade, you look down on a
>   winding pool.
> Its lotuses have just opened; among
>   them grow water-chestnuts,
> And purple-stemmed water-mallows
>   enamel the green wave's surface.

Fig. 20 Procession of horses and chariots on painting from Mawangdui tombs

Height 99 cm, length 219 cm
Hunan Provincial Museum

This image of a grand procession from the tomb of Li Xi, the second Marquis of Dai under the Han dynasty, who died c. 168 BC, suggests the splendors of the rich Chu region.

We are also told that in the palace:

> There are loggias and covered walks
> for exercising beasts in …
> Here you may gallop or amble at
> leisure, or hunt in the spring-
> quickened park.[2]

Clearly, therefore, in the rich and fertile Chu state, approximating to present-day Hunan Province in the Yangtze valley (fig. 20), where these chants were composed, the ruler's palace included pleasure-gardens and a hunting-park.

In the nature of things, early historical records are mostly concerned with the activities of rulers and the highest level of the elite, so the little that we do know about gardens at this time is concerned with those of this social group, not of any gardens that might have belonged to commoners. Given the autocratic nature of early Chinese rulership, it is also most likely that only the ruler and his closest associates controlled enough land to be able to turn it to other than productive use.

Emperor Qin Shihuang and His Gardens

More information about gardens—although still only at the upper levels of the elite—is available once China had entered the imperial period, beginning with the conquest and unification of the various "warring states" by the state of Qin in 221 BC. We know something about the imperial gardens and parks which the ambitious First Emperor of Qin (Emperor Qin Shihuang, 259–210 BC) established or expanded during his reign (221–210 BC). The Shanglin or Supreme Forest Park south of the Qin capital Xianyang (close to present-day Xi'an, Shaanxi Province) was one of these. It appears to have been a park which already existed in the time of earlier rulers of the state of Qin, but was enhanced by the First Emperor to fit his new status as ruler of all China.

The First Emperor is also said to have used the water of the nearby Wei River to form a lake (the Orchid Pool) in which he had constructed replicas of the islands of the immortals together with sculptures of whales or other sea creatures. His self-identification with the immortals was enhanced by covered corridors built through his parks to connect his various palaces, so that he could move about unobserved, appearing in one place or another as if by magic. Many of the buildings and other features within the imperial parks were located to reproduce the positions of stars in the sky, thus drawing on the powers of astronomy or astrology to enhance the emperor's own power. All this must have added greatly to the impression of the emperor's authority.

Early records indicate that inside the First Emperor's magnificent tomb (fig. 21)—to one side of which the Terracotta Warriors were first uncovered in the 1970s—a facsimile of the whole known world was created: "They used mercury to create rivers, the Jiang (Yangtze), the He (Yellow River), and the great seas, wherein the mercury was circulated mechanically. On the ceiling were celestial bodies and on the ground geographical features."[3] Given the lavish retinue of soldiers, chariots, entertainers, and others which accompanied the Emperor in death, it is likely that the "world" within his tomb also included a representation of the

gardens or parks which he had enjoyed in life. Indeed, according to a writer who lived shortly after the fall of the Qin, describing its construction, "The middle of the tomb became a pleasure ground [for the dead emperor], and the upper part [i.e. the exterior of the tomb mound] a mountain forest." However, the tomb mound itself (unlike its surroundings) will not be excavated until Chinese archeologists are confident that they have the technology to conserve its contents successfully, so we will have to wait to see any surviving physical evidence of the appearance of the Qin Emperor's gardens.

Fig. 21 The tomb of the First Emperor of Qin is located to the east of the present-day city of Xi'an, Shaanxi Province. The Qin capital Xianyang was to the north of Xi'an. The tomb mound shown here, probably containing replicas of the emperor's parks and gardens, was surrounded with buried images of footsoldiers and charioteers (the famous Terracotta Warriors) as well as musicians, acrobats, and other entertainers.

The Nanyue Palace Garden

An interesting garden from around 200 BC, of which physical evidence does survive, was located far from China's heartland, in what is now the city of Guangzhou, although at that time it was very much the wild south. The kingdom of Nanyue, incorporating parts of present-day Guangdong, Guangxi, Fujian, and the island of Hainan, and extending into what is now northern Vietnam, was set up after the fall of the Qin by a former Qin military commander, who declared himself king of an independent realm. The kingdom lasted from 204 to 111 BC, although latterly it became a tributary state of the Han dynasty which replaced the Qin.

Excavation of the King of Nanyue's tomb and palace in the 1990s uncovered part of the palace garden or park, thought to be similar in layout to those of the Qin and presumably modelled on what the king and his courtiers knew of the Qin palace gardens in far-away Xianyang. A long, narrow pebble-paved channel which seems to have been carefully structured to create a flow of rippling water wound through the Nanyue Palace garden. This channel ended at a crescent pool to the east, which was probably covered by a semi-circular structure (fig. 22). The pool was found to contain the remains of many turtles: from early times in China, turtles have been seen as magical creatures and symbols of long life, since they live to a great age. The markings on their shells and the use of their plastra (the underpart of the shell, below the turtle's belly) in early divination rituals also associated them with esoteric knowledge. These mystical qualities no doubt account for their presence in the palace garden pool, which is a reminder that royal and imperial gardens were not just sites for the display of worldly power and for enjoyment and entertainment but were also intended to put their owners in contact with supernatural forces.

Shanglin Park

The association of gardens and parks with supernatural as well as worldly power can be seen very clearly in the Han dynasty which

Fig. 22 Excavated remains of Nanyue Palace garden

In the foreground is part of the crescent-shaped pool. The watercourse which ran into it, built of worked stone blocks and paved with pebbles, can be seen in the middle distance.

followed the Qin. The Han, which established Chang'an as its capital, close to the Qin capital Xianyang, was a relatively stable regime which lasted much longer than the Qin. As a result, many more detailed historical records, literary works, and visual images survive from this period, including several "prose-poems" or "rhapsodies" (*fu*) on the Shanglin Park and other imperial landscapes written by court poets. It is also a time in which we know a little about non-imperial gardens, although still at an elite level.

In the time of the great emperor Han Wudi (the Martial Emperor of Han, r. 141–87 BC), the Shanglin Park was greatly enlarged from its proportions under the Qin. As befits court poetry, composed for the glory of the ruler, the poems on the Shanglin Park tell us more about the mental image of the imperial precincts than about what it actually looked like or comprised. The magniloquent descriptions suggest a landscape that was intended to impress and overawe the spectator with the power and majesty of the emperor. The names of exotic birds, beasts, and plants imply that the emperor's dominion extends to the farthest and most obscure parts of the world. Parts of the park, perhaps even the grounds of the palace itself, functioned as a menagerie where wild beasts were kept for the interest and amusement of the emperor

Fig. 23   Scene from the *Admonitions of the Instructress to the Court Ladies* after Gu Kaizhi (348–409)

Ink and color on silk
Dimensions of the complete handscroll: height 25.5 cm, length 377.9 cm
British Museum, London

The scroll illustrates a text composed in the 3rd century AD, giving instruction on the behavior suitable to ladies of the imperial court. This scene depicts the courageous Lady Feng helping to fight off a bear which escaped from the royal menagerie, the Tiger Enclosure, and was about to attack the emperor himself in the palace. This incident, which occurred around 35 BC, shows the danger of keeping wild beasts within the palace grounds!

and his family (fig. 23).

Less poetic and more factual records indicate that the Shanglin Park operated very much as a productive estate. Rushes were grown to supply the many buildings with the matting and cushions on which people sat (chairs were still unknown in China). There were buildings distributed throughout the area of the park, some for residence and recreation, but many for productive use. There were even parts of the park in which copper or bronze was mined and worked. One set of buildings was used as a hothouse to grow exotic plants and trees from the south, including oranges and lychees. Assuming this was entirely enclosed, it must have had windows to allow sunlight in. Glass was not used for windows in China until the 18th century at the earliest, and windows were "glazed" with translucent paper or silk. Given that paper was still at an early stage of development in the Han dynasty, the windows of this hothouse were probably made of silk. The cultivation of semi-tropical plants in northern China, with its cold and dry winters, demonstrates that Chinese gardeners already possessed a high degree of skill in horticultural techniques.

There was said to be stabling for 300,000 horses within the Shanglin Park, though whether this number represents full capacity or the actual number of horses is not clear. These horses would be used in hunting and also for military purposes: organized hunts often functioned as training for military maneuvers. The quantity of manure produced would certainly benefit the fertility of the soil in those parts of the park which were cultivated as flower or vegetable gardens!

Construction and maintenance of the royal park was carried out at least partly by corvée laborers. (Corvée was the system whereby adult male commoners were required to spend part of the year laboring on public works projects as a form of non-monetary taxation.) It was possible to buy oneself out of corvée obligations by payment of a fee, and such fees helped to support the great cost of the Han military campaigns in Central Asia. Towards the end of the Former or Western Han (206 BC–AD 25), as these costly military advances brought economic troubles, the emperor allowed farmers to take over parts of the Shanglin Park to grow essential crops; by the time the capital moved to the east, most of the park had gradually been turned to agricultural use and its former glory was no more (fig. 24). The royal parks constructed around the eastern capital, Luoyang, in the Later or Eastern Han (AD 25–220) were smaller and less splendid than those of Chang'an.

The Weiyang Palace Garden

The Weiyang Palace, the main palace complex of the Western Han dynasty, was established by the first Han emperor (Han Emperor Gaozu, r. 202–195 BC) in the south-western corner of the capital Chang'an, as the main seat of government and residence of the imperial family.

While the parks outside the walls of Chang'an seem to have been largely masculine spaces, the Weiyang Palace within the city contained a garden or park in its south-western part which adjoined both the emperor's residence to the east and that of the empress and other palace women in the north-western quadrant and was available for the use of these women. Additionally, the park had other functions: the pond or lake within

Fig. 24   Wall tile (rubbing)
Eastern Han
Length 45.6 cm, width 39.6 cm
Sichuan Museum

The upper part of the tile shows a duck-hunt, with archers aiming at flying birds, beside a pond in which fish are swimming and lotus growing. This might resemble some of the hunts which took place within the imperial parks of the Han dynasty. The lower part of the tile shows a harvest scene such as occurred once the Shanglin Park was taken over by farmers.

it, fed from a much larger lake to the southwest of the city, stored water for palace use (for drinking, cooking, washing, and also for fire prevention), and it also contained a space for ritual agriculture in which the emperor, in his role as intermediary between heaven and earth, performed the annual ceremony of ploughing the soil to symbolize the start of the growing season. This ceremonial act by the reigning emperor was maintained into the early twentieth century, as long as the imperial system survived.

Three Celestial Islands in One Pond

Some of the Han emperors were particularly interested in the quest for immortality (fig. 25). In pursuit of this quest, parts of the imperial gardens were designed to resemble the legendary islands of the immortals, believed to exist in the Eastern Ocean, and sometimes identified with Japan or the Ryukyu islands. The dwelling of the immortals was thought to consist of three islands, Fangzhang, Yingzhou, and Penglai. Hence, the placing of three islands, or even just three rocks, in a pond or lake was intended to reproduce this magical realm, in the hope that the immortals would be deceived into mistaking the imperial gardens for their home, and would come to reveal the secrets of immortality to the emperor himself.

The first certain appearance of the "three islands in a pond" occurred in the Grand Liquid Pond (*Taiye chi*) created in the garden of the Martial Emperor's splendid Jianzhang Palace, which occupied a part of the Shanglin Park just outside the western wall of the capital Chang'an; this was also an early example of a garden positioned behind (i.e. to the north of) the main residential buildings, which became the standard layout in later times. Ever since the Han dynasty, it has been

Fig. 25   Bronze "Boshan" incense-burner
Western Han
Height 23.9 cm, diameter 10.1 cm
Palace Museum, Beijing

The upper part of this incense-burner takes the form of the "Boshan" or archetypal magic mountain. The holes allowed the incense smoke to escape and perfume the air, looking like mist wreathing the mountain. The decoration shows beasts in combat, hunters shooting at birds, figures of immortals, and a bird, probably representing the Red Bird of the South, perched on the peak of the mountain. The supporting figure, sitting on a mythical beast, enhances the magical atmosphere. The imperial parks of the Han dynasty emulated such mystical mountains.

customary to include in Chinese gardens—and in gardens of those cultures strongly influenced by China, such as Japan, Korea, and Vietnam—three islands or rocks in a pond to allude to the home of the immortals and the possibility of the garden's owner achieving transcendence (see fig. 38 on page 35).

Gardens of the Elite

The long and relatively stable rule of the Han dynasty (interrupted by a brief interregnum under the control of an imperial relative in AD 9–24, followed by the removal of the capital from Chang'an eastwards to Luoyang) allowed time for an interest in the creation of gardens and parks to spread from the imperial family to the social elite, the aristocrats whose forebears had supported the first Han emperor in establishing his dynasty, and even to some who had grown wealthy by other means. In the Eastern Han, centralized imperial power was challenged by powerful local families whose power and wealth was based on manorial landholdings; this ultimately helped to provoke the fall of the Han dynasty.

The few records that survive indicate that such non-imperial gardens resembled those of the emperor, though on a lesser scale. At this stage there was no stylistic difference between imperial and non-imperial gardens, as later became the case. Indeed, they could be interchangeable: one of the few early non-imperial and non-aristocratic gardens

Fig. 26 Decorated earthenware tile from Han-dynasty tomb, Zhengzhou, Henan Province

Height 119 cm, width 49 cm, thickness 15 cm
Henan Museum

The decoration shows the grounds of a large house or palace. Within the gate (upper right) are growing stylized trees, formed by a stamp repeatedly impressed into the clay, while in front of the gate are more trees as well as exotic birds, both inside and outside a walled enclosure.

Fig. 27 Rubbing of Eastern Han relief carving from the east wall of the niche in Shrine 1, Wu Family shrines, Wuzhaishan, Shandong Province

The carvings in the shrines show scenes from history and mythology, but also reflect daily life at the time. In the second register here, we can see winged people (immortals) in what appears to be a garden or park with trees, including what is possibly a weeping willow. Although this scene represents the realm of the immortals, it also gives us an idea of how gardens and parks were conceptualized at the time.

Fig. 28   Western Han tomb tile

Height 46.5 cm, width 38.2 cm, thickness 6.8 cm
National Gallery of Victoria, Melbourne

The pheasant-like birds shown between the two rows of stylized trees in the upper register of this tile suggest that the scene may represent a wooded park where game birds are kept for hunting, and the tiger may also be kept in a park for hunting, rather than living (or dying) in the wild.

of which we know—that of the wealthy Yuan Guanghan around 100 BC—was confiscated by the government when Yuan faced criminal charges, and the animals and plants which he had cultivated there were removed to the imperial Shanglin Park.

Some ideas of how gardens and parks were conceptualized at the time can be gleaned from stone-carvings and from molded or impressed clay tiles used in construction of the tombs of the elite (fig. 26). One panel of carved stone from the famous Han-dynasty Wu Family shrines in Shandong Province (fig. 27) shows several trees in close proximity to a group of winged immortals, two of whom are flying; this suggests that groves of trees, perhaps in a park-like setting, were felt to have a numinous quality (as indeed they did and do in many cultures). The clay tiles used in tombs were often impressed with repeated stamps showing features such as trees within an enclosing border. Another

Western Han tomb-tile (fig. 28) shows in its upper register three pairs of pheasant-like birds sandwiched between two rows of conifer-like trees, suggesting a park intended for hunting or amusement, and in the lower register a man attacking a tiger with an axe, above another row of the same trees made with the same or a similar stamp.

The evidence that survives about parks and gardens in this early period implies, though does not prove, that they were mostly for the use of the imperial family and the upper levels of the elite, and that even at this level they were used mainly for productive and practical purposes, while at lower levels of society, if gardens existed at all, they were there to supply the need for food and other material goods.

CHAPTER TWO
SIMPLICITY AND SPLENDOR
FROM THE PERIOD OF DISUNION TO THE TANG

After the Han dynasty finally collapsed in AD 220, the socio-political structure of China changed considerably. Gone was the unified empire, which split up into a number of smaller, contending polities, similar to though more short-lived than the "Warring States" which had preceded the Qin unification four and a half centuries earlier. This period of disunion, often called the "Six Dynasties" (222–589), includes the "Three Kingdoms" (220–280), "Sixteen Kingdoms" (304–439), and "Northern and Southern Dynasties" (420–589), which gives a sense of the confusion endured by China's population. The most important of the Northern and Southern Dynasties were the Jin (265–420) in the south and, in the north, the Northern or Tuoba Wei (386–534), founded by the Tuoba clan of the Xianbei, a Turkic or Mongolian ethnic group from the steppes, who became increasingly sinicized. As a result of the relative stability of these two regimes, the culture of the period is often referred to as Wei-Jin culture.

Gardens and Retreat to the Countryside

The contending polities throughout the period of disunion could be unstable internally as well as externally, and life became dangerous for the elite class of officials who had previously enjoyed relatively predictable careers under the Han. Buddhism had by now made its way from South Asia to China along the routes established by trade (fig. 29), and the new religion appealed to both elite and commoners with its promise of release from suffering. The indigenous Chinese tradition of Daoism also held out hope of escape from the

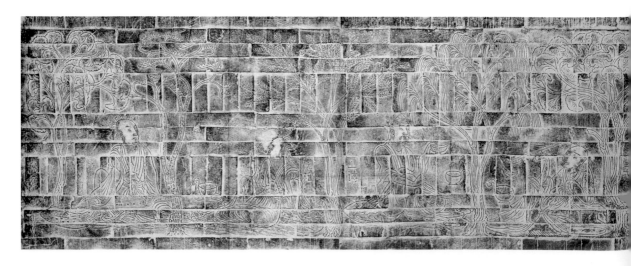

Fig. 29 A double tree shrine
Northern Liang period (397–439)
Cave 275, Mogao Caves, Dunhuang
Dunhuang Academy

The pair of stylized trees enclosing the shrine niche are a non-Chinese feature in the visual culture of the Dunhuang cave temples on the Silk Road. Many new visual elements entered Chinese art along with the introduction and spread of Buddhism. In Buddhist art, the bodhi tree under which the Buddha attained enlightenment and the parks in which he preached form important settings for images of the Buddha.

mundane world through transformation into an "immortal" or transcendent being. Many of the elite turned away from striving for official position and political influence and took up a pose of leisured eccentricity, often accompanied by drunkenness. The desire to retreat from the world into a garden-like sanctuary is

epitomized by the 3rd-century "Seven Sages of the Bamboo Grove," seven members of the elite famed for their poetry, love of wine, eccentricity, and Daoist leanings. They are depicted in molded wall tiles or bricks from an Eastern Jin (317–420) tomb near Nanjing, drinking and playing musical instruments, seated among trees of different kinds (fig. 30). Our knowledge of what gardens at this time were actually like still depends on such hints in works of visual art and literature.

Shi Chong (249–300), a wealthy and powerful official under the Jin dynasty, included a brief description of his luxurious Golden Valley Garden (*Jingu yuan*) in a preface which he wrote for a collection of poems written during a gathering in the garden. The garden or estate was ten *li* (about three miles) outside the town where he was posted at the time. Evidently it was a productive estate,

Fig. 30 The Seven Sages of the Bamboo Grove (with the addition of one earlier historical figure) in a moulded brick relief
Nanjing Museum

The relief shows the sages enjoying wine and music in a garden or park setting. The fact that they were thought suitable for depiction in a tomb only about one hundred years after their own time indicates how rapidly the seven became almost legendary figures. The setting also suggests how closely they were associated with natural surroundings, in this case trees rather than bamboo.

Fig. 32 *Letter Presenting Oranges* after Wang Xizhi

Palace Museum, Taibei

This example of the great calligrapher's style (a close copy—no originals survive) is a short letter accompanying a gift of oranges, presumably grown on the Wang family's estate. The letter simply reads: "I present to you three hundred oranges. Since there has not yet been a frost, no more are yet obtainable." Low temperatures cause the sugar content of the fruit to rise, so after a frost they taste sweeter.

Fig. 31 *Golden Valley Garden* (1732)
Hua Yan (1682–1756)
Hanging scroll, ink and color on paper
Height 178.9 cm, width 94.1 cm
Shanghai Museum

The luxury and extravagance of Shi Chong's Golden Valley Garden remained a popular topic of art and literature throughout Chinese history. Here the 18th-century artist Hua Yan, one of the Eight Eccentrics of Yangzhou, depicts the garden as though it were the elegant retreat of a Ming or Qing literatus. Shi Chong is seated on the ground, leaning on an armrest and listening to music played by his favorite concubine Green Pearl.

as it had arable land, a plot of medicinal herbs, watermills, fishponds, and various domesticated animals including sheep, pigs, hens, ducks, and geese. In addition, it provided a pleasing leisure environment, with springs of fresh water, fruit trees, bamboo,

pines, and caves: "everything that would delight the eye and satisfy the mind."[4] Later writers and artists regarded the Golden Valley as the epitome of splendor and luxury in a garden (fig. 31).

A slightly later individual who—although not directly associated with a specific garden himself—had a profound influence on later garden culture was the calligrapher Wang Xizhi (303–361) (fig. 32). He is most famous for his preface—modelled on that written by Shi Chong—to the *Orchid Pavilion Collection*, a collection of poems written on an occasion in the year 353 when a number of literati gathered at a place named the Orchid Pavilion outside the city of Shaoxing (Zhejiang Province) to drink and compose poetry. They are believed to have sat beside a winding stream and floated wine-cups along it: as each wine-cup reached a participant, he had to compose a verse. In later times, winding "streams" were deliberately constructed in gardens for the purpose of playing this game in memory of that famous occasion (fig. 33). The seminal figure of Wang Xizhi is often referred to in other ways also, such as by naming a pond "Ink Pool" in memory of the pond in which he was said to have washed his calligraphy brushes. His son Wang Huizhi (338–386) also contributed to later garden culture through his fondness for bamboo, saying of the plant, "How can one live one day without this gentleman!" As a result, bamboo was often referred to as "this gentleman," and many gardens included a "This Gentleman Pavilion" surrounded by bamboo.

Many of the social elite who had rejected officialdom found it appropriate to pose as simple farmers, since in the Confucian four-level social hierarchy, farmers were the next rank down from officials (above artisans and merchants). One who did this was the great poet Tao Qian (also known as Tao Yuanming, 365–427), another seminal figure in Chinese garden culture. He is famous for

Fig. 33   Meander for floating wine-cups in the Elegant Jewel Pavilion, Tanzhe Temple, Beijing

As a substitute for a real stream, winding channels such as this were carved in stone and installed in the gardens of temples and palaces as well as private gardens. Friends would gather around them to drink and compose poetry in memory of Wang Xizhi's gathering at the Orchid Pavilion.

his poems extolling the pleasures of a simple life in the countryside, in a genre which became known as "pastoral" or *tianyuan*, literally meaning "fields and gardens." In fact, of course, members of the elite such as Tao would not lower themselves to real agricultural labor, so directing the creation and cultivation of gardens in which to lead their leisured and eccentric lives became an appropriate substitute. Tao's devotion to the chrysanthemum—which because it blooms in the autumn is associated with long life and healthy old age—meant that this flower became a favorite in gardens of the elite through the ages. Simply growing chrysanthemums in one's garden became a way of claiming spiritual kinship with the great poet (fig. 34). The "pastoral" way of life

Fig. 34   *Tao Yuanming and Chrysanthemums* (detail)

Attributed to Qian Xuan (late 13th century)
Ink on silk
Dimensions of the complete album leaf: height 21.8 cm, width 20.6 cm
Freer-Sackler Gallery, Washington DC

Originally attributed to a 13th-century painter, this is now thought to be a work of the Qing dynasty. The subject of Tao Yuanming enjoying chrysanthemums has been a popular one throughout the history of Chinese painting.

established a pattern of literati culture which in many ways persisted, or was reinvented, throughout the following centuries, even though Chinese society changed over time almost beyond recognition.

Enjoyment of the countryside became one of the ways in which the elite could escape from social pressure even if they remained in office, and in this period we find in written records a new attitude to landscape. It is seen not so much as a mysterious manifestation of cosmic powers, but as something with its own esthetic value to be appreciated by sensitive observers. It is no coincidence that this period saw the beginning of landscape painting, which subsequently became a major genre of art, closely tied to the development of garden design. Landscape could also be regarded by Buddhist believers as a visible manifestation of the Buddha's nature. A distinguished poet, almost contemporary with Tao Qian, whose work enables us to understand more about attitudes to landscape in this period was Xie Lingyun (385–433). Unlike Tao Qian's focus on gardening and agriculture, Xie's poetry is

more concerned with the wider and wilder landscape, particularly that of his extensive estate in what is now Zhejiang Province. In his lengthy "Rhapsody on Dwelling in the Mountains" he describes this estate in great detail, stressing its completeness and sufficiency for his needs as a "recluse." This emphasis forms a sharp contrast with the detachment from material things which is a tenet of the Buddhist faith. Xie was nevertheless a devout Buddhist and is often described as a poet of "landscape Buddhism," the manifestation of Buddhist ideals through the forms of the landscape (fig. 35). His poetry is likely to have contributed considerably to the incorporation of Buddhist ideas into the design of later gardens.

Monastery and Temple Gardens

With the rise of Buddhism as well as the increasing prominence of Daoism in the period of disunion before the Tang dynasty, a new form of garden appeared, the monastery or temple garden. Since in urban settings many such institutions were originally private houses which a wealthy donor had made over to a religious purpose, their gardens are likely to have been similar in style to the private gardens of the elite. We can gain some idea of the gardens of urban Buddhist monasteries from the descriptions in *A Record of the Monasteries of Luoyang*, written towards the middle of the 6th

Fig. 36   Mural painting of *Constructing Pavilions and Planting Trees*
Northern Zhou dynasty (557–581)
Cave 296, Mogao Caves, Dunhuang
Dunhuang Academy

The richly decorated pyramidal ceiling of Cave 296 includes many narrative images intended to encourage virtuous behavior among the Buddhist believers who frequented the cave temples of Dunhuang. Among a series of good deeds including tending to the sick and digging wells to provide water, we find this scene showing people planting trees whose shade and fruit would refresh weary travelers, and constructing garden pavilions as part of a temple complex.

century, shortly after the city of Luoyang had ceased to be the capital of the Northern Wei dynasty. The author, Yang Xuanzhi (?–c. 550), had been an official there and knew the city well. We can see that, although the monastery gardens were intended to form a peaceful and refreshing environment, with "dark trees and green waters," where "pine, bamboo, orchid, and iris overhung the steps"[5] (as Yang says of the Jingming Monastery, founded around 500), the ponds were also used to grow aquatic plants such as water-chestnuts for food and reeds to make rush matting, the soil to grow fruit and vegetables, and the flowing water to operate mills to grind grain or husk rice. The gardens therefore formed an integral part of the monastic economy, while they were visited not just by monks and worshippers but also by urban pleasure-seekers attracted by the pleasant environment. Even in areas far from the Chinese cultural heartland the creation of gardens was seen as desirable and even as an act of religious piety: one of the murals in the Buddhist caves at Dunhuang on the central Asian Silk Road shows a scene of a garden being created, with trees, water, paths, and pavilions (fig. 36).

Fig. 37   The spectacular scenery of Mount Lu has inspired visitors and residents from the time of the Buddhist patriarch Huiyuan in the 4th century to the present day. The Tang poet Li Bai (701–762) compared its waterfall to the Milky Way flowing down from heaven; within later gardens, waterfalls were sometimes given names recalling Mount Lu and Li Bai's poem. The Song poet Su Shi (1037–1101), looking round at all the different views the mountain offered, famously observed that "one cannot see the true face of Mount Lu, just because one is within this mountain." Part of the art of Chinese garden design is to ensure that a visitor within a garden can never see the entire garden, so that it maintains its air of mystery.

Founders of a monastery or hermitage often preferred it to be remote from the secular world: this meant going into the hills and mountains, and finding a site with a reliable water supply and with plentiful timber for construction and for firewood, as well as rocks for foundations and paving. In such a site the monastery would naturally be surrounded with fine scenery, which must have helped to influence ideas of garden design. The famous Buddhist monk Huiyuan (334–416), who founded the White Lotus Society on Mount Lu (Kuanglu, Lushan), attracted many secular followers who took up residence on the mountain, which is well-known for its beautiful scenery (fig. 37). It is likely that this environment had a significant influence on people's ideas of what was desirable to include, reproduce, or represent within a garden setting.

In the Tang dynasty, Buddhism played a significant role in garden culture. Empress Wu Zetian (624–705), one of the most remarkable and notorious rulers of the dynasty and the only woman ever to have ruled China in her own name (r. 690–705), made use of the religion to enhance her imperial aura—she styled herself an incarnation of the future Buddha Maitreya—and to combat her officials who, as Confucians, disapproved of a woman holding power. The power of Buddhism in the Tang was not limited to the imperial court but extended throughout society. Many Buddhist monastic institutions became extremely wealthy and effectively controlled their local economies. Since religious institutions were exempt from paying tax, rich land-owners often made over parts of their property to Buddhist monasteries for tax reasons (while continuing to enjoy the use of the property during their lifetimes). One result of this was that gardens became an increasingly important feature of Buddhist monasteries and temples, and while Buddhism played a more important role in garden culture generally, private gardens also had an influence on monastic gardens. Eventually the economic dominance of institutional Buddhism provoked a backlash from the Confucian state: many monasteries were closed down and Buddhist believers were persecuted. Although Buddhism never regained the same degree of secular power, it retained its hold on the hearts and minds of the population, both elite and non-elite, and its role in garden culture.

The association of gardens with Buddhist monasticism also had a powerful effect in other areas under Chinese cultural influence, such as Korea and Japan, as can be seen

Fig. 38 Garden of the Kenninji Temple, Kyoto, Japan

The lines raked into the gravel represent waves on the ocean, and the rocks on the left represent the three islands of the immortals from Chinese legend. The representation of the three islands became an almost essential part of Chinese gardens from early times, and was adopted in Japan when Chinese monks introduced Buddhism to Japan together with ideas about how temples and gardens should be laid out.

to this day (fig. 38). Tang dynasty garden culture influenced Japan in particular, not only through its links with Buddhism but also through other Chinese beliefs, such as Daoist conceptions of the islands of the immortals (touched on in Chapter One in the mention of the role of the "three celestial islands in one pond" in other Confucian-influenced cultures), and the teachings of *fengshui* or geomancy. Although Buddhism had been known in Japan from at least the 6th century onwards, it was during the Tang

that Chinese Buddhism became particularly influential there. The travels of monks between China and Japan (fig. 39), as well as those of merchants and diplomatic envoys, conveyed ideas about both Buddhism and garden culture to Japan, and Buddhist-influenced gardens started to be created there. Chinese gardens thus had a profound and long-lasting influence on the development of garden culture in Japan. Of all East Asian garden traditions, that of Japan has probably had the most impact around the world today, yet much of it can be traced back to China in the Tang dynasty.

Fig. 39 The memorial hall for the monk Jianzhen (688–763), a Buddhist missionary from China to Japan in the 8th century, at the Daming Monastery in Yangzhou (Jiangsu Province), has been designed in Tang dynasty style, to show how Chinese architecture and design influenced Japanese Buddhist temples. The monastery as an institution dates back to the mid-5th century, while the memorial hall was built in 1973, after the establishment in 1972 of diplomatic relations between Japan and the People's Republic of China.

Imperial Gardens

The small scale and unstable nature of the states established during the period of disunion generally meant that their rulers had neither resources nor leisure to devote to the creation of "imperial" gardens or parks. Nevertheless, some of them attempted to do so, and it appears from written records that, rather than following the new esthetic of private gardens, rulers tried to reproduce the magnificence of Han-dynasty imperial gardens, with what success we do not know. It would seem, though, that unlike the extensive Shanglin Park, most imperial gardens in this later period were either inside or very close to the capital city; it is likely that the rulers did not have sufficient control over the countryside to spread their parks further afield.

After the period of disunion had been brought to an end by reunification under the short-lived Sui dynasty, to be followed by the highly successful and long-lasting Tang dynasty, garden culture flourished. The most significant act of the Sui (apart from the reinstatement of the government examinations pioneered by the Han for the recruitment of officials) was the development of the Grand Canal, particularly the section between Yangzhou on the Yangtze and Luoyang, the second capital of the Sui, on the Yellow River. Under the second Sui emperor, Yangzhou became the second most important city of the empire thanks to its vital position at the junction of the Yangtze and the Grand Canal, and began its rise to fame as a wealthy and luxurious garden city. The notoriously extravagant Emperor Yang of Sui (569–618, r. 604–618) constructed a complex of palaces and gardens there known as the Labyrinthine

Fig. 40   The Guanyin Temple in Yangzhou is reputed to stand on the site of Emperor Yang of Sui's "Labyrinthine Tower."

Tower (*Milou*) to house his many concubines: it was said to be so elaborate that it was impossible to find one's way out (fig. 40).

The succeeding Tang dynasty built on the infrastructural and organizational foundations laid by the Sui. Society in the Tang experienced the start of the transition from an aristocratic to a bureaucratic form of government which was consolidated in the Song dynasty, but the Tang dynasty represents the last flowering of aristocratic culture in China, while at the same time nurturing the beginnings of the type of literati garden which came to dominate the garden culture of late imperial China.

The splendors of the Tang imperial court included many impressive gardens and parks. The early Tang emperors seem to have tried to rival the splendors of the Han imperial parks. However, although the parks were still used for hunting and other forms of military exercise, there is evidence of a new attitude towards the birds and beasts which they contained. Perhaps because of the increased influence of both Buddhism and Daoism from the period of disunion into the Tang, there was more of a sense that animals should be left to get on with their lives, albeit confined within a park, rather than have them ruthlessly subordinated to human will and subject to the mass slaughter of the Han hunting displays. Greater importance was placed on the flowers, plants, and fruit in the imperial gardens, which often came as tribute to the court from distant parts of the empire, and which in turn might be used in imperial rituals, for example as offerings in the dynastic cult.

Within imperial garden culture, women played a substantial role (fig. 41). We know of a garden belonging to Princess Changning (680–after 728), which seems to have been located in the countryside outside the capital, Chang'an (present-day Xi'an). The garden was celebrated in verses by a female courtier, Shangguan Wan'er (664–710), who was the private secretary of Empress Wu Zetian. As she did with Buddhism, Empress Wu Zetian used garden culture as a way to consolidate her authority, once claiming that peonies bloomed in the imperial gardens in response to her personal orders, thus demonstrating her own numinous powers.

The court of the Tang Emperor Xuanzong, also known as the Glorious Emperor of Tang (Tang Minghuang, r. 713–756), was dominated by one particular woman, the Honored Consort Yang (Yang Guifei, see fig. 9 on page 9). The besotted emperor is said to have been particularly charmed by the sight of his consort emerging from her bath in the Palace of Splendid Purity or Huaqing Palace (*Huaqing gong*), a hot-spring resort for the imperial court on the northern slopes of Mount Li to the east of the capital. Archeological excavations on the site of the Palace of Splendid Purity in the 1980s–1990s have revealed much about the layout of this palace-garden-spa complex. The area around the original hot spring source, in the south-

Fig. 41 *Court Ladies Adorning Their Hair with Flowers* (detail)
Attributed to Zhou Fang (730–800)
Ink and color on silk
Dimensions of the complete handscroll: height 46 cm, length 180 cm
Liaoning Provincial Museum

The crane, dog, and smaller court lady are additions to the scroll from a separate painting. A connoisseur who owned the scroll in the early Qing attributed it to the Tang painter Zhou Fang, but there is no reliable provenance for it before the Southern Song, when it was in the palace collection, so it may show a later concept of Tang court activity. The court ladies are shown gathering flowers from the magnolia bush on the left to place in their hair.

eastern quadrant of the Tang complex, was already in use by the First Emperor of Qin in the 3rd century BC, but the development under Emperor Xuanzong covered a much larger area. In addition to courtyard gardens in the central area, there were more expansive gardens for viewing plantations of prunus blossom and other plants in the western and eastern sections, as well as accommodation and performance spaces for the court theatrical troupe, and pitches used for open-air sports such as polo, a great favorite of the Tang court (fig. 42). As well as indoor bathing-pools such as the emperor's Nine Dragon Bath and Lady Yang's Lotus Blossom Bath, there seem to have been outdoor pools for the use of lesser members of the court, sometimes planted with lotuses, which were a theme in the decoration of the buildings (fig. 43). There were also vegetable gardens to supply the court during their autumn and winter sojourns at the hot springs, and it is possible that the geothermal heat was exploited to prolong the growing season of melons and other fruits.

Fig. 42   Mural painting from the tomb of Li Xian (Prince Zhanghuai, 655–684) in the Tang imperial Qianling Mausoleum near Xi'an, Shaanxi Province
This wall painting shows polo being played in the palace grounds. All the riders shown here are men, but women are also known to have played.

Gardens of Tang Scholar-Officials

Generally speaking, Chinese society and government in the Tang dynasty was still organized on aristocratic lines, as it had been in previous dynasties. However, the increased complexity of society arising from the prosperity brought by the Silk Road trade routes (among other factors) meant that governing the empire increasingly required intelligence, education, and expertise rather than the advantages of birth and wealth. Although the use of government examinations for the recruitment of officials would not become fully institutionalized until the succeeding Song dynasty, this method of recruitment, based at least nominally on education and merit rather than inherited social position, was used more and more during the Tang dynasty. The educated officials who emerged from this system seem to have developed a strong sense of class identity (despite some bitter factional disputes) which was manifested in a distinctive literati culture expressed in

Fig. 43   Floral tiles with lotus-blossom center, excavated at the Tang-dynasty Palace of Splendid Purity hot springs complex.

gardens as much as in literature and art.

One change which took place in garden culture as a result of the rise of the scholar-official class in the Tang was a new interest in small gardens. Previously gardens—imperial and aristocratic—had been valued for their size and splendor. Now the rising class of officials who were not necessarily wealthy (at least not in comparison with the aristocracy: they were certainly rich beyond the wildest dreams of most people in the country) promoted the idea that a relatively small garden could still have esthetic value. Nevertheless, some wealthy scholar-officials still maintained substantial estates, such as the poet and painter Wang Wei (699–759 or 701–761) with his Wheel River (Wangchuan) estate outside the capital, Chang'an (fig. 44). Although Wang was from a well-off land-owning family, this estate was a property which he purchased for himself, not a family inheritance. Wang was a devout Buddhist, and in the intervals of a generally successful official career he lived on his estate, writing, painting, and carrying out Buddhist devotions. It is clear from his poems and from a surviving letter to his friend Pei Di that he had a deep love of nature and landscape, and saw in them manifestations of Buddhist truth. From a sequence of poems which he wrote about sites on his estate, we know the names of many

Fig. 44 *After Wang Wei's "Wheel River"* (detail)
Guo Zhongshu (c. 910–c. 977)
Ink and color on silk
Dimensions of the complete handscroll: height 29 cm, length 490.4 cm
Palace Museum, Taibei

This section of the scroll shows the part of the Wheel River estate named Deer Enclosure, a Buddhist reference.

of them: some are simply descriptive (Lake Pavilion, South Hill), while others embody references to Daoism or Buddhism. Probably the best known of these poems is one on the site named Deer Enclosure or Deer Park, in reference to the park near Varanasi (Benares) where the historical Buddha preached:

> Hills empty, no one to be seen
> We only hear voices echoed—
> With light coming back into the
>   deep wood
> The top of the green moss is lit
>   again.[6]

Here the emptiness of the hills reflects the absence of attachment which is the aim of the Buddhist believer, while the "light" is that of Buddhist enlightenment.

Another aspect in which the Tang dynasty differed from earlier times was a new appreciation for different types of landscape, resulting from the posting of scholar-officials to different parts of the country. The long-lasting stability and prosperity of the Tang dynasty meant that many areas which had

Fig. 45 The scenery of Lake Tai near Wuxi is an example of the beautiful, well-watered, gentle Jiangnan landscape, which so impressed the Tang dynasty officials who were posted to this area that they tried to replicate it in their gardens in the north.

been only tenuously connected to the Chinese heartland in the Yellow River valley were now firmly attached to the empire. In fact, a process of change was beginning which came to fruition only in the subsequent Song dynasty: the tilting of the balance of population and economic prosperity from the Yellow River plains in the north to the Yangtze valley and delta in the south. It was the Jiangnan area—the region of the Yangtze delta and the fertile lands to the south of the Yangtze's lower reaches—which made the greatest impression on the itinerant officials of the Tang (fig. 45). One of China's best-loved poets, Bai Juyi (772–846), was governor of Hangzhou in the early 820s. He had grown up in the relatively arid north, and the beautiful, well-watered landscape of the Hangzhou area made such a profound impression on him that when he retired to Luoyang in the north he endeavored to recreate the Jiangnan landscape in his garden there (fig. 46). He planted a pond with lotuses and had his concubines go out

in small boats to pick them, harking back to early poems called "lotus-picking songs." The eroticization of the Jiangnan landscape derived from tales of the glamorous south in earlier times: it became a commonplace to compare the beautiful West Lake (*Xi hu*) of Hangzhou to the beautiful Xi Shi who was sent by the 5th-century BC King of Yue (the ancient kingdom in which the West Lake was located) to seduce and bring about the downfall of King Fuchai of the state of Wu (based around today's Suzhou). The era of the Southern Dynasties in the 5th and 6th centuries AD, which mostly had their capitals in Jiankang (now Nanjing) on the Yangtze River, was also remembered as an era of glamour and *la dolce vita*.

Fig. 46 The Bai Causeway on Hangzhou's West Lake is said to have been constructed on the orders of Bai Juyi when he was governor of the city. It is noted for its blossoming peach-trees in spring and its green willows in summer. Bai and other northern officials who served in the area were charmed by the landscape and vegetation of the West Lake.

Penjing (Bonsai) and Lake Rocks

Art that survives in the tombs of the Tang imperial family shows landscapes and plants of the time, as well as the emerging art of *penzai* ("potted planting") or *penjing* ("potted landscapes"), the Chinese origin of Japanese *bonsai*. However, if this was an art form which began in the imperial household (fig. 47), it was soon taken up by the rising class of scholar bureaucrats.

Of course we still know very little about gardens of the literati class other than what is described in literature, both prose and poetry (very few authentic paintings survive from the Tang period), but one aspect that we can see clearly, closely related to the interest in *penjing*, is a growing focus on rocks—placed in gardens or as "scholar's rocks" in the study—both for their esthetic appeal and for their metaphorical function as images of the scholar himself: ugly and awkward in shape and thus rejected by the majority, but valued by the perceptive for their inherent integrity. Because of factional conflict in government (a constant throughout Chinese history), officials or would-be officials often felt themselves to be misunderstood and cast aside for inadequate reasons: thus the metaphor of the "useless" or "unappreciated" rock became a commonplace in their complaints about lack of success in their careers. But an enthusiasm for rocks seems still to have been confined to relatively few, very wealthy officials, and regarded by most literati as an extreme form of eccentricity.

Two scholar-officials who became notorious both for their obsession with rocks and gardens and for their intense mutual hostility as leaders of opposing factions at court were Niu Sengru (780–848) and Li Deyu (787–850). Niu Sengru managed to amass a vast collection of Lake Tai (Taihu) rocks in his garden in Luoyang, as we know both from his own poetry and from an essay

Fig. 47 Detail of a mural (AD 706) in the tomb of the Tang prince Li Xian (cf. fig. 42 on page 38), showing an attendant carrying a *penjing* or potted landscape. The dish holds a combination of rocks and plants.

written by his friend Bai Juyi, who tries to justify Niu's "addiction" to these objects. It seems that many if not most of Niu's rocks were gifts from other officials, particularly those who were posted in the Jiangnan area where the rocks originated, and that they were transported all the way to Luoyang through the government transportation system. Niu's petromania thus made him vulnerable to accusations of corruption. His rival Li Deyu was less interested in rocks but was obsessed with plants. He owned a "mountain villa" at Level Springs (Pingquan) outside the city of Luoyang, with a garden full of rare flora, and wrote a "Record of the Plants and Trees of My Mountain Villa at Pingquan," chiefly consisting of a list of the plants, as well as some rocks, with their places of origin. More eloquent than this record is his "Exhortation to My Children and Grandchildren about the Mountain Villa at Pingquan," in which he insists that his descendants must preserve the villa and its garden intact: "Whoever sells the villa at Pingquan will be disowned by me. Whoever sells one piece of rock or a single plant will not be considered a good member of the family."[7] In later garden literature, Pingquan became a symbol of the transient nature of gardens and the vanity of human wishes, since within not much more than a century the garden had been abandoned and only two rocks remained.

CHAPTER THREE
LITERATI ESTHETICS
SONG DYNASTY

As we saw in the previous chapter, the Tang dynasty marked the start of the transition from aristocratic government to the bureaucratic government which became such a notable feature of the Chinese political system, and this transition also led to the emergence, among the social class who formed the scholar-official elite, of a distinctive literati culture which incorporated particular attitudes to gardens.

New Trends in Song Society Influence Gardens

The Song dynasty, which established a stable government in 960, after about half a century of conflict between short-lived regimes following the fall of the Tang, took up and firmly institutionalized the bureaucratic system of government. This led to the dominance of government by men who defined themselves primarily by their level of education rather than by the advantages of birth.

This social change, in its turn, promoted the development of neo-Confucian philosophy and ideology, arising partly from a backlash among the governing class against the ideological and economic dominance of Buddhism in the Tang dynasty. The sophisticated cosmology of Buddhism challenged the proponents of traditional Confucian ethics, primarily concerned with the here-and-now and the practicalities of social relationships, to develop a more metaphysical underpinning. What emerged from this was the "study of the Way" (*daoxue*) or the "study of principle" (*lixue*, referring to the principles of the cosmos), which are the Chinese terms for what Western scholars have named neo-Confucianism. This ideology still has a strong influence on Chinese social ethics and behavior. There were many other distinctive features of the Song period which have led some historians to regard it as the beginning of the "early modern" era in China, many centuries before Europe could be described as "early modern." These features also had a range of impacts on garden culture.

One of these features was increasing urbanization. Cities expanded, at the same time as they became less rigidly controlled than they had been under the Tang. A higher proportion of the population lived in towns or cities (although urban dwellers still formed only a small proportion of the population as a whole). Because of the relaxation of controls on commerce, more economic activity became concentrated in cities rather than in rural market towns. The Song capital shifted from the carefully planned Tang capital, Chang'an, with its enclosed sub-divisions, to Bianliang (modern Kaifeng), also in the Yellow River valley but much further east. Bianliang was already a thriving commercial city with excellent transport links to other regions; its vibrant urban life is vividly

depicted in the famous painting *Along the River during the Qingming Festival* (*Qingming shanghe tu*) by Zhang Zeduan (1085–1145) (fig. 48). It has been estimated that by the late 11th to early 12th century, the population of Kaifeng was as large as 1.5 million, making it one of the greatest cities in the world at the time.

Monetization of the economy increased, so that a growing number of the population exchanged goods and services for cash, rather than relying on self-sufficiency or barter; an active handicraft production system developed to replace home-made utensils with those made by specialists. The shift of population to the more fertile south and the concomitant development of double-cropping (new strains of rice allowed for the growing of two crops a year rather than just one) led to economic growth which increased disposable income, at least for those living above subsistence level. The flourishing commercial economy led to neglect of military preparedness, and the non-Han Jurchen people who had established the Jin ("Golden") dynasty (1115–1234) to China's north-east took advantage of this to invade and conquer North China, which

Fig. 48 *Along the River during the Qingming Festival* (detail)

Zhang Zeduan
Ink and color on silk
Dimensions of the complete handscroll: height 24.8 cm, length 528 cm
Palace Museum, Beijing

This section of the scroll shows, in the foreground, a wineshop in which customers can be seen drinking in the upper storey, overlooking the courtyard which contains trees and presumably other garden elements; there are also trees growing between the wineshop and the riverbank, suggesting a garden-like environment for the customers to enjoy. Other commercial activity is taking place outside, and the river is thronged with vessels transporting goods and passengers.

they ruled from the mid-12th to the mid-13th century. The Song court fled southwards and established a "temporary" capital at Lin'an (modern Hangzhou) where they remained for another one and a half centuries as the Southern Song dynasty, until the Mongols conquered the whole of China. This governmental move southwards followed the southward shift which was already taking place in the balance of the economy and population of China.

The Rise of the Literati Garden

The fact that, with the growth of urbanization, the Song-dynasty scholar-official class (whether or not they were actually in government office) preferred to live among the amenities of cities rather than on country estates meant that their gardens might have to be quite small, at least compared to what was possible in rural areas (fig. 49). An increasing value placed on smallness and simplicity, combined with the growing commitment of the literati to an esthetic of elegance, plainness, and "blandness" (*dan*), gave rise to the distinctive "scholar-garden" style which came to fruition

in the late Ming dynasty. Nevertheless, some literati still chose to live in the countryside. While many wrote poetry or prose about their rural or urban gardens, we know of only one Song-dynasty literatus who made a painting of his garden: this was Li Gonglin (1049–1106), who painted his "Mountain Villa" in the Longmian (Sleeping Dragon) Mountains of present-day Anhui Province. Li had spent the 1070s living in reclusion in his Mountain Villa, but created this painting (which now survives in a number of close copies) at a time in the 1080s to 1090s when he was working as a government official in the capital, Kaifeng. We have no way of knowing how far the painting resembled the real-life mountain villa and its surroundings, but it gives us an idea of how a land-owner at the time might have conceptualized his estate, or idealized it in memory, and how he would have made use of the site for leisure activities (fig. 50).

Fig. 49   Stone stele with map of Pingjiang City
Southern Song dynasty
Height 284 cm, width 145 cm
Suzhou Museum of Inscribed Stone Tablets

This shows the dense layout of the city of Suzhou (then known as Pingjiang or "Calm River") in the Southern Song period. At least one garden-like enclosure is visible in the south of the city (the bottom of the map), surrounding an official building. Suzhou at this time was a flourishing commercial city, famous for its handicrafts and its *douceur de vivre*.

Self-Representation in the Garden

The autobiographical focus of written garden descriptions which had come into being in the Tang dynasty now makes an impact on Song visual art. This was not an entirely new phenomenon, since it is clear that in his "Mountain Villa" painting Li Gonglin was consciously referring to the Tang-dynasty poet and painter Wang Wei's depiction of his own Wheel River estate (see fig. 44 on page 39), as well as to Lu Hong's (fl. 713–742) "Thatched Hut" (*Caotang tu*), of which Li actually painted a copy. Li's "Mountain Villa" painting depicts landscape in a very different way from the great Northern Song (960–1127) court painters such as Guo Xi (c. 1020–c. 1090) (see fig. 64 on page 56). The handscroll format presents us not with a synoptic view but with a series of vignettes, inspired by map-making and geomantic diagrams as well as by the "higher" art of landscape painting, showing us the owner and his guests enjoying different features or scenes within the garden landscape. Very few buildings are shown, and mostly on an unrealistically small scale; it is known that in Song gardens the buildings tended to be few and widely dispersed, quite different from the density of garden structures in later dynasties. Li's Mountain Villa had twenty named sites (by no means all buildings), as we know both from this scroll and from a set of poems

Fig. 50 *Mountain Villa* (detail)
After Li Gonglin
Ink on paper
Dimensions of the complete scroll: height 28.9 cm, length 364.6 cm
Palace Museum, Taibei

This part of the scroll shows a mountainous area of Li's estate. On the right, a servant is boiling a kettle for tea, while a young boy carries a tray of tea-cups rather perilously across stepping stones to a group of gentlemen on the other side of the stream. In the center, three gentlemen sit contemplating a waterfall, which is labelled as "Hanging Clouds Linn" (*Chuiyun pan*). Further to the left, servants are preparing a picnic, apparently for the group of men, including two monks and a boy, seated on a terrace listening to a lecture given by a gentleman holding a feather fan.

written by his friend Su Che (1039–1112).

An aspect of Song literati gardens which carried through to those of later dynasties was an increased emphasis on literary, and to a lesser extent artistic, allusion in the garden. Because of the shared educational and cultural background of the literati, allusions to the literature and the cultural heritage of the past could be used to convey to the visitor aspects of the garden owner's outlook on life. In preceding dynasties such allusions do not seem to have been a major component of gardens, which were more concerned with the demonstration of wealth and social standing than with cultural and ideological positions. Names given to gardens or garden features prior to the Song were

usually no more than simple descriptions of what the features consisted of or where they were located, such as "West Flat Bridge" or "Pavilion on Middle Islet" in the Tang poet Bai Juyi's garden in Luoyang.

This new use of allusion is well illustrated in the garden of the historian and senior official Sima Guang (1019–1086), who developed his Garden of Solitary Enjoyment (*Dule yuan*; fig. 51) in the empire's second city, Luoyang, while excluded from the government based in the capital, Kaifeng, as a result of conflict with the then leading official Wang Anshi (1021–1086). The name of the garden itself is an allusion to a passage in *Mencius*, in which the philosopher urges King Hui of Liang (r. 370–319 BC) to share his enjoyment of his garden and other pleasures with his people, as a true king should do. Sima Guang claimed in his prose account of his garden that he was too humble and insignificant to be able to share the enjoyment of it with others and therefore he enjoyed it in solitude, although as we will see this was not entirely the case. Seven features within the garden—five buildings, a terrace, and a herb-garden—were named in honor of seven scholars, poets, or recluses of the past, and Sima wrote a set of seven poems ("The Garden of Solitary Enjoyment: Seven Songs") specifying who was associated

Fig. 51 *The Garden of Solitary Enjoyment* (detail)
Qiu Ying (c. 1494–c. 1552)
Ink and color on silk
Dimensions of the complete scroll: height 32 cm, length 1290.2 cm
The Cleveland Museum of Art

The scroll shows Sima Guang's Garden of Solitary Enjoyment as visualized centuries later by the Ming painter Qiu Ying. This detail shows Sima Guang in (on right) the Dallying with Water Gallery, named in honor of the Tang poet Du Mu (803–853), who had a Dallying with Water Pavilion, and (on left) the Reading Hall, named in honor of the Han scholar Dong Zhongshu. Qiu Ying seems to have followed Sima Guang's description of the garden quite closely, although some elements reflect Ming rather than Song garden style.

with each feature and why Sima particularly admired him. For example, in the first poem, on "The Reading Hall," which he describes in his prose "Account of the Garden of Solitary Enjoyment" as containing 5,000 volumes of books, he explains that the Han-dynasty Confucian scholar Dong Zhongshu (179–104 BC) studied the classics so devotedly that he ignored the garden of his dwelling, and as a result of his scholarship he was able to establish Confucianism as the leading ideology of the Han dynasty. It is not hard to draw the conclusion that, in identifying with Dong Zhongshu, Sima Guang is laying a claim to be a true Confucian unlike those officials currently in power.

Sima Guang was by no means the only

literatus to emphasize Confucianism in the naming of his garden and its features: similarly, we know of a garden simply named the North Garden which had a "Hall of Intention" divided into sections with names such as "Seek Humaneness," "Establish Rightness," and "Depend on Trustworthiness," all alluding to fundamental Confucian virtues. Compared to the subtle allusions embodied in many garden feature names in the late imperial period, these names are still fairly direct: it does not require extensive cultural knowledge to grasp their meaning. This was also the case in the Plot of Joy (*Lepu*), the garden of the calligrapher Zhu Changwen (1039–1098), which included features such as the Hall of Penetrating the Classics, the Zither Terrace, on which Zhu played his zither (Zhu wrote an important treatise on this instrument, the *qin*), the Ink Pool, alluding to Zhu's interest and skill in calligraphy (and embodying a reference to the great 4th-century calligrapher Wang Xizhi), and a high point called Mountain View (there was a terrace with the same name, alluding to the poet Tao Qian, in Sima Guang's garden). Although the Plot of Joy was quite a large site, there were not many buildings in it; this architectural sparseness seems to have been a feature of Song gardens, as we noted in relation to Li Gonglin. Zhu's own essay describing his garden forms a "self-portrait"

in much the same way as Li Gonglin's depiction of his Mountain Villa. This type of self-representation appears much more self-conscious and in-depth than the inchoate self-representation in the gardens of the Tang literati, and will be taken even further in the later imperial period.

Song and later neo-Confucianism placed much emphasis on the concept of self-realization or self-actualization: the idea that the virtuous man will strive to become his "best self." Confucian names for garden features and the associated use of the garden for self-representation or "autobiography" therefore expressed the owner's aspiration to self-actualization, further consolidating the shared cultural and philosophical mentality— what has been referred to as a "shared body of ethical norms"—of the newly-powerful scholar-official class. The idea also takes hold that what makes a garden admirable and memorable is not the garden itself, which might be small and insignificant, but the reputation of the garden's owner. This was the reason for the fame of Sima Guang's Garden of Solitary Enjoyment, as we are told by the Song writer Li Gefei (1045–1106), who wrote a *Record of the Celebrated Gardens of Luoyang*, containing brief descriptions of many of the best known gardens in this cultural center shortly before the fall of the Northern Song.

Gardens Open to Visitors

The Garden of Solitary Enjoyment, as we know from other accounts, was opened to the public on certain days of the year, particularly at the lunar New Year, at the cost of a tip paid to the gatekeeper. One story relates that so many people wanted to visit this garden because of the fame of its distinguished owner that the gatekeeper made a lot of money; one day Sima Guang was surprised to find a new pavilion in his garden, which it turned out that the grateful gatekeeper had paid for out of his gains! Whether or not this is a true story, it indicates that in this period private gardens could be accessible to members of the public who were not acquainted with the owner.

Another well-known anecdote connecting a famous literary figure with visits to a garden concerns the Southern Song poet Lu You (1125–1210). Having been forced by his domineering mother to divorce his beloved first wife, he later visited the Shen

Below

Fig. 52   The Shen Garden, Shaoxing, Zhejiang Province

Archaeological excavations have shown that there was a garden on this site in the Song dynasty, and it has been identified with the Shen family's garden in which Lu You is said to have encountered his former wife. The garden has been reconstructed in recent years and does not necessarily bear any resemblance to the appearance of the garden in Lu You's time.

Fig. 53   *Children at Play in an Autumnal Garden*
Su Hanchen (fl. mid-12th century)
Hanging scroll, ink and color on silk
Height 158.3 cm, width 108.1 cm
Palace Museum, Taibei

This detailed and realistic scene of a boy and girl playing in a garden reminds us that gardens were the setting for family life as well as for literary and cultural activity. Gardens provided women and children of elite families with an outdoor but private environment for enjoyment, relaxation, and play. This scene is dominated by an impressive "strange rock," while the hibiscus and chrysanthemum flowers show that the season is autumn.

family garden in his hometown of Shaoxing, Zhejiang Province, now identified with a garden there which excavations have shown to date back to the Song dynasty (fig. 52). After a chance meeting there with his former wife and her second husband, Lu was moved to compose a song lyric which he inscribed on the garden wall, a lyric which became one of the best known and loved of any from the Song dynasty. His ex-wife later responded by writing a lyric to the same tune (Song-dynasty lyrics were usually written to pre-existing tunes or metrical patterns). It is not known whether this romantic story has any basis in reality, but aside from showing that it was considered normal for men to visit private gardens without necessarily calling on the owner, it suggests that this was also possible for elite women, who are often thought to have been confined to the home once the somewhat repressive social norms of neo-Confucianism had taken hold in society.

Women and Gardens

Compared to the Tang dynasty and to the later Ming and Qing, we know little about the part played by women and children in Song-dynasty garden culture (fig. 53). It is interesting to note, though, that the site of the Plot of Joy referred to above was originally purchased in the 1040s by Zhu Changwen's paternal grandmother, Ms. Wu, rather than by a male relative. From the work of another Song poet we can learn something of what gardens meant to women at the time: this was Li Qingzhao (1084–c. 1151), usually regarded as China's greatest woman poet. She was the daughter of Li Gefei, the author of the *Record of the Celebrated Gardens of Luoyang*. Li Qingzhao and her husband were forced to flee south when the north came under the control of the Jin dynasty, losing most of their extensive collection of books and works of art. Li's husband died young, and many of her later poems recall the happiness of their married life. Her poems often depict a garden environment which provides the setting for the poet's daily life (fig. 54) as well as reflecting her emotional life ("Pear blossoms are about to fall, / But there's no helping that").[8]

Fig. 54 *Lady at Her Dressing Table in a Garden*

Su Hanchen
Fan painting, ink, color, and gold on silk
Height 25.2 cm, width 26.7 cm
Museum of Fine Arts, Boston

This image is a variation on the theme of "beauties in a garden": here there is only one "beauty," with her maidservant, and rather than posing elegantly she is getting on with daily life, applying her make-up or adjusting her coiffure. Although her back is turned to the spectator in this private moment, her face is cleverly revealed in the mirror.

"Strange Rocks"

An aspect of literati garden culture which developed greatly from the situation in the Tang dynasty, and which was imitated and further developed in subsequent centuries, was the enthusiasm for "strange rocks." As we have seen, in the Tang dynasty an enthusiastic interest in rocks (petrophilia or petromania) was confined to relatively few literati, who had to be quite wealthy to indulge this passion. In the Song dynasty, petrophilia seems to have become much more widespread among the scholar-official class, and to have been regarded less as a weird individual quirk and more as an accepted component of the literati personality. Only very extreme devotion or eccentricity seems to have left a lasting impression: for example, the painter Mi Fu (1051–1107) became known for his deep respect for a particularly impressive rock, bowing to it and addressing it as "elder brother" (fig. 55). The great poet and calligrapher Su Shi (also known as Su Dongpo, 1037–1101), who like his brother Su Che was a friend of Li Gonglin, had a difficult official career, being sent to various remote postings and even sentenced more than once to internal exile; he made a point of collecting rocks wherever he travelled, though he was not always able to take them with him (fig. 56). From a practical point of view, most of his collection had to be made up of rocks which were small enough to be easily transportable, and as he became a cultural model for later literati to emulate, this must have prompted a growing interest in smaller rocks which could be displayed indoors as well as outside, in fact what are now usually referred to as "scholars' rocks" (fig. 57).

Fig. 55 *Mi Fu Bowing to the Rock*
Chen Hongshou (1598–1652)
Hanging scroll, ink and color on silk
Height 112 cm, width 50 cm

The late-Ming mannerist painter Chen Hongshou depicts his fellow-eccentric from the Song dynasty, Mi Fu, paying his respects to an extremely elaborate Lake Tai rock, as others look on in some surprise.

Lin Youlin (1578–1647) was a late-Ming rock collector from Huating in Jiangsu, which is close to the source of many of the rocks most prized by collectors. The woodblock-printed illustrations in his book, which was named after the Lin family's garden, are said to be based on his own paintings. This rock, named "Mount Jiuhua within a Jar" (*Huzhong Jiuhua*), is described as one which was seen by Su Shi in someone's garden. Su Shi wrote a poem in praise of it, but when he returned to the garden eight years later, the rock had already been removed by another collector. Su's poem indicates that the rock was named after the real Mount Jiuhua ("Nine Blossoms") because it had nine peaks.

Gardens of the Emperors

Despite the prominence of literati gardens in the written record, imperial gardens remained very important in the Song period, although with one change: the great hunting parks of previous dynasties were not continued, probably because of increased cultivation of land. The proliferation of grand imperial gardens within the walls of the capital, as well as private gardens both in the capital and elsewhere, must have led to increasingly crowded housing within cities, and thus to the spread of urbanization to the suburban areas beyond. At the same time, maintenance requirements for these parks and gardens provided employment for many specialists and laborers, and also supported a lively horticultural trade. Some Buddhist monasteries around the Southern Song capital even specialized in the cultivation of particular plants, such as azaleas or osmanthus.

A glimpse of gardens enjoyed by palace ladies in the period following the end of the Tang or in the very early Northern Song is given by a painting by a 10th or 11th century artist illustrating the sad story of the Tang Emperor Xuanzong's love for his concubine

Fig. 57 "Scholar's rock" (19th century)

Overall height (with base): 61.9 cm
Metropolitan Museum of Art, New York

As well as the large rocks installed in gardens, the Chinese literati also valued smaller rocks which could be placed on a carved stand (as here) or incorporated in *penjing* and displayed in a study or other indoor space. These natural rocks (sometimes with some artificial assistance) resemble mountainous scenery and recall the islands of the immortals. In idle moments, the owner can imagine himself wandering among their contours and caverns and encountering mystical beings.

Fig. 58 *Palace Banquet*
(detail)

Anon. (10th or 11th century)
Ink and color on silk
Dimensions of the
complete hanging scroll:
height 161.6 cm, width
110.8 cm
Metropolitan Museum of
Art, New York

The tragic love story of the
Tang Emperor Xuanzong
and his concubine
Honored Consort Yang
inspired many works of
art and literature from the
late Tang dynasty onwards.
Here a tryst between the
lovers is about to take place
during the evening of the
Double Seventh Festival.
In the buildings of the
palace gardens, the palace
women are preparing for
an elaborate banquet.

Honored Consort Yang (fig. 58). The ladies
are holding a feast to celebrate the festival of
the 7th night of the 7th lunar month, the one
night of the year when the celestial lovers, the
Herdboy and Weaving Maid stars (Altair and
Vega), are united. Parts of a garden area can be
seen in the foreground, with rocks, flowers,
trees, and decorative balustrades. The nature
and quality of this painting suggests that it
may be the work of a court artist, and it may
therefore reflect palace life in the artist's own
time rather than in the Tang.

Palace gardens were important not only
to the imperial family throughout the year,
but also to the general public in the capital:
it appears that most of the imperial parks
of the Northern Song capital were opened
to the public on at least some occasions,
whether recurring annual festivals or specific
individual celebrations, and thus served as a
kind of public park. They also functioned,
as in previous dynasties, as sites where
military maneuvers could be practiced: this
was particularly the case with the lakes,
which were used for naval displays and mock
battles, especially the Reservoir of Metal's
Luster (*Jinming chi*) to the west of the capital
city (fig. 59). The opening of the imperial
gardens was intended to awe and impress
the populace, but the populace turned it
to their own uses, no doubt enjoying the
spectacle of imperial ritual or naval exercise,
but also making use of the opportunities on
offer for the consumption of commercially
available food and drink, gambling, theatrical
and acrobatic performances, or encounters
with prostitutes. Thus the newly expanded
mercantile activities of the Song economy
invaded the usually enclosed space of the
imperial grounds.

However, there was one imperial garden
that was never supposed to be open to the
public, and yet it became the best known,
indeed the most notorious. The Song
dynasty had reached a height of cultural
brilliance under the Emperor Huizong
(1082–1135, r. 1100–1126), who was himself
a gifted painter and calligrapher (fig. 60).

He was, however, less gifted as a ruler, and it was his extravagance and the rapacity of his subordinates in acquiring exotic plants and unusual rocks for his gardens which were blamed for the downfall of the dynasty. Particular blame fell upon the so-called "North-East Marchmount" (*Genyue*) or "Mountain of Long Life" (*Shoushan*), constructed in Huizong's reign. As the name suggests, it was located to the north-east of the imperial palace. This direction was associated in geomantic (*fengshui*) lore with fertility and the birth of sons: the garden, which mainly featured a substantial artificial hill,

Wang Zhenpeng worked as an official in the Yuan dynasty palace, where he painted this scroll for the Mongol princess Sengge Ragi (c. 1283–1331), a noted art collector. It represents a regatta held on the Jinming Pond of the Northern Song imperial palace in Kaifeng to celebrate the Dragon Boat Festival, as described in *A Dream of Splendors in the Eastern Capital* (*Dongjing menghua lu*), a Southern Song memoir of the Northern Song capital in its heyday, two centuries before the date of this painting.

Emperor Huizong, though rather a failure as a ruler, was a gifted artist, particularly in the "flower and bird" style as seen here. His sensitive observation of nature was no doubt trained by his familiarity with the plants and birds of the imperial gardens. On the right of the painting appears his coded signature as "The One Man under Heaven" (*Tianxia yiren*).

was built in the hope that it would enable the Emperor Huizong to father many potential heirs (he did). It is the garden most closely associated with the notorious "Flower and Rock Convoy," the system for requisitioning for imperial use rare plants and rocks from all over the empire, which was exploited by imperial servants and brought great hardship to the victims of their extortions. When the Northern Song capital was besieged by the conquering Jin army in the winter of 1126–1127, stones from the North-East Marchmount were used as cannon-balls, while the cold and hungry inhabitants and defenders of the city felled the trees and tore down the buildings in the park for firewood, and slaughtered the "thousands" of deer in the park for food. Thus the park, constructed between 1117 and 1122, lasted a mere decade from conception to utter destruction. It is not surprising that it became a byword for fatal imperial extravagance (fig. 61).

Once the Song court had fled south and taken up residence in Hangzhou, the Southern Song emperors naturally required appropriate palaces and gardens. They had the advantage of starting construction in what

Fig. 61 *Auspicious Dragon Rock*
Emperor Huizong of Song
Handscroll, ink and color on silk
Height 53.9 cm, length 127.8 cm
Palace Museum, Beijing

This Lake Tai rock may well have been one of those brought to the imperial palace by the notorious Flower and Rock Convoy. The inscription written by the emperor in his characteristic "thin metal" (*shoujin*) calligraphy describes the rock's position in the imperial garden and praises its impressive and auspicious form.

was already a much admired scenic landscape centered on the West Lake (fig. 62). The main imperial palace, including a large park, was constructed on Phoenix Hill in the southern part of the walled city of Hangzhou, then known as Lin'an ("Temporary Peace"). Most of the park was situated on the northern slopes of the hill, overlooking West Lake, so it benefited from a relatively cool micro-climate. The park had a wealth of plants as well as various structures in which the emperor and his family could sit or stroll to take the air and admire the view. The

Fig. 62   The West Lake, Hangzhou, Zhejiang Province
Hangzhou was the site of the Southern Song capital. The lakes, rivers, and gently rolling hills of the south-east are very different from the environment of the Northern Song capital in the Yellow River valley, and had a strong influence on Southern Song landscape painting, which itself influenced garden esthetics.

vegetation in this relatively warm and humid climate must have made quite a change from what the imperial family had been used to in the Northern Song capital Kaifeng. Other "traveling palaces" (*xinggong*: the name for imperial residences away from the main palace) and imperial gardens dotted the shores of the West Lake and the northern bank of the Qiantang River which flows south of the city; these allowed the emperor and his entourage to enjoy views of this celebrated landscape from many different angles. The Southern Song emperors often gave the gardens of their traveling palaces to favored ministers for their private use: this suggests that there was considerable overlap in the style of imperial and private gardens at this time.

Imperial gardens might be echoed on a much smaller scale in the gardens of government offices. Such gardens existed in the Northern Song, as we know from an 11th-century anecdote about the blooming of a rare type of herbaceous peony in the garden of a government office in Yangzhou. There is also evidence from the Southern Song, when in 1257 the prefect of Yangzhou, Jia Sidao (1213–1275), who subsequently became a very senior official at court, much reviled for his role in the dynasty's collapse, reconstructed and enlarged an abandoned garden attached to the prefectural residence. The reconstructed garden seems to have been of considerable size, since there were numerous buildings, a lake large and deep enough for boating on, and a hill high enough to allow a view beyond the city. The description of it suggests that it resembled a literati-style garden rather than anything too "official." It was intended for the private enjoyment of government officials, perhaps for the prefect and his friends and family alone, but the public were allowed to visit it to admire the blossom during the spring, much like the practice in the private gardens of Luoyang in the Northern Song.

Gardens of the Academy

A third type of garden, distinct from private literati gardens and imperial or official gardens, was that of academic institutions. With the dominance of government by officials educated in the Confucian tradition—and the reassertion of Confucianism after the pre-eminence of institutional Buddhism throughout much of the Tang academies for the education of aspirant officials became very important. Institutions such as the Yuelu Academy in what is now Changsha, the capital of Hunan Province, had the resources to develop a "campus" landscape which provided a pleasant environment for students and teachers (fig. 63). Such a designed landscape also linked the built environment to the wider landscape around: the Yuelu Academy, for example, is nestled in what were originally uncultivated mountain surroundings. Similarly, the White Deer Grotto (*Bailu dong*) Academy, founded in the late 10th century and revived by the great philosopher Zhu Xi (1130–1200) in the late 12th century, was situated on the slopes of the scenic Mount Lu, long a retreat for Daoist hermits and Buddhist monks (see Chapter Two). During the

Fig. 63   A covered walkway in the grounds of Yuelu Academy, now part of Hunan University, Changsha, Hunan Province. A collection of calligraphy engravings on stone is inset into the walls of the walkway for visitors to study as they stroll through the campus garden.

Southern Song, academies were more often constructed closer to urban areas, particularly in places associated with great scholars of the past. The success of such academies was often attributed to the accumulation of *qi* (vital energy) occasioned by the conformation of the landscape, enabling the development of outstanding scholars and administrators.

Such campuses and their adjoining landscapes were intended not only to form a pleasant environment, but also to inspire the students, through observation of the variety of plants, the movement of water, the cycle of the seasons, to a deeper understanding of the natural world and the entire cosmos. As the noted neo-Confucian thinker Cheng Yi (1033–1107) expressed it, in the "investigation of things" (*gewu*, the way to comprehend the moral universe), "every blade of grass and every tree possesses pattern [*li*, also meaning principle] and should be examined." Thus the students at the academy would advance their knowledge and also their moral character.

Analysis suggests that the design and content of such academic gardens was somewhat different from that of private gardens, being geared towards shared enjoyment of the "natural" (albeit designed) environment and its use for discussion between teachers and students and as a form of teaching aid, rather than towards enjoyment by an individual owner and expression of such an owner's personal interests. At the same time, it would not be unreasonable to suppose that the experience of academic gardens might influence the tastes and preferences of former students when they came to develop their own gardens.

Fig. 64 *Early Spring*
Guo Xi
Hanging scroll, ink and color on silk
Height 158.3 cm, width 108.1 cm
Palace Museum, Taibei
Guo Xi was an official painter in the Painting Academy at the Northern Song court.

The Influence of Landscape Painting and Tea Culture

The governmental move southwards consequent on the fall of the Northern Song led not only to political change but also to significant cultural changes, particularly in landscape painting and thus also in the type of landscape which was valued and emulated in garden design. Northern Song painting, particularly the court painting produced in the imperial Painting Academy, is noted for grand, impressive landscapes of towering mountains, inspired by mountainous landscapes north of the Yangtze River, which fill the picture space (fig. 64). In the Southern Song, by contrast,

Fig. 65 *Boating near Lake Shore with Reeds*

Attributed to Ma Yuan
Album leaf, ink and color on silk
Height 23.8 cm, width 24.1 cm
Museum of Fine Arts, Boston

Composed in Ma Yuan's characteristic "one-corner" style, this landscape painting reflects the gentle, well-watered scenery of south-east China where the Southern Song government took refuge from the Jin invaders. This change from the harsher landscape of north China undoubtedly affected attitudes towards garden esthetics.

the landscapes depicted tend to be those of the Jiangnan region, south of the Yangtze, and particularly those around the Southern Song capital and the nearby West Lake, with lower, more rolling hills and expansive bodies of water. Often these landscape paintings would be composed with large parts of the picture space left almost blank, giving a sense of openness and relaxation, as seen in the paintings of Ma Yuan (1190–1235), known as "One-Corner Ma" (*Ma Yijiao*) from the characteristic composition of his landscapes (fig. 65). It is most likely that Southern Song gardens shared this sense of openness and restraint in design; certainly the much greater water resources in southern China, compared to the north, would offer the opportunity for more extensive use of water in the design of southern gardens.

Gardens and landscape in Song China were closely interwoven with other aspects of

culture, particularly the culture of tea, which rose to great importance in the life of the literati and of Buddhist monks. Tea originated as a medicinal drink but became widely used for general drinking during the Tang dynasty. It was a particularly useful drink for Buddhist monks, for whom the consumption of alcohol was forbidden: as a stimulant, tea enabled the monks to stay alert through long hours of meditation or religious ritual. By the Song dynasty, tea-drinking had spread to all classes in society, while "tea contests" or tea-tasting, which often took place in a garden setting, became a way for the leisured class to demonstrate their cultural superiority and connoisseurship. Many of the ceramic wares for which the Song is particularly famous took the form of tea bowls (fig. 66), whose

Fig. 66 Jian-ware black-glazed tea bowl

Height 7 cm, rim diameter 12.8 cm
Palace Museum, Taibei

Song-dynasty ceramics are world famous. Tea bowls such as this, with their black glaze setting off the white froth on the surface of the tea, would be used for the appreciation of tea in a garden setting. The streaky pattern of this glaze is known as "hare's fur."

dark color was designed to contrast with the creamy white froth of the tea, which at this time was prepared by whisking powdered leaves in hot water (this is still practiced in the Japanese tea ceremony, which arrived from China along with Buddhism).

The cultivation of tea-bushes was often undertaken by Buddhist monasteries, many of which were located in mountainous areas which were particularly suited to growing tea, primarily for their own use. There was a high demand for tea, not just among the Chinese population but also for the government to maintain peace with China's potentially aggressive neighbors or to exchange for commodities such as high-quality horses, used in transport and warfare, which could not be bred within China (fig. 67). As tea could not be grown in central Asia, the inhabitants were very willing to accept Chinese tea in exchange for their products delivered in "tribute" to the emperor (the so-called tribute system was really a disguised form of state commerce). The main state production of tea in the Song dynasty took place in Fujian (still a major tea-producing area). It is no coincidence that the most prized "Jian ware" tea bowls were also produced in this region. The demand for tea led many land-owners to turn over part of their estates to tea production, often for commercial purposes, but sometimes for production on a more modest scale within a garden for their own household use. The fact that tea was grown in relatively wild and remote areas meant that it was seen as a "natural" product and therefore particularly good for both spiritual and physical health, in much the same way as medicinal herbs gathered in the wild are believed to be more efficacious than those which are deliberately cultivated.

The development of tea-plantations on a large scale naturally had an effect on the landscape. Such links between economic and esthetic values in the landscape can be seen in other contexts also, even in the visual arts. Li Gonglin's scroll of his "Mountain Villa" which we have already discussed can be seen not only as a celebration of the beauty and seclusion of his estate, but also of his ownership of this desirable property. We will see in the next chapter how the link between landscape painting and property developed during the Yuan dynasty.

Fig. 67 *Five Tribute Horses* (detail)
Li Gonglin
Ink and color on paper
Dimensions of the complete scroll: height 29.5 cm, length 225 cm
Tokyo National Museum

Li Gonglin, the owner and painter of the villa in the Sleeping Dragon Mountains, was also noted for paintings of horses. Here we see one of a group of five stallions presented in "tribute" to the Song emperor by China's north-western neighbors, who were able to breed much finer horses on their extensive grasslands than could be raised in China, where most farmland was arable. The groom leading this horse has central Asian features.

CHAPTER FOUR
THE POLITICS OF RECLUSION
YUAN DYNASTY

In studies of the history of Chinese gardens, the Yuan period (1279–1368) when China was under Mongol rule is often ignored, yet it can be seen as pivotal in the development of late-imperial garden culture. In particular, it was important in the widespread adoption and advancement of the concept of eremitism or reclusion in relation to literati garden culture.

Literati Gardens

As we have seen, the idea of becoming a hermit in one's garden first appeared in the Tang dynasty and became more widely adopted in the Song, stimulated particularly by the intense and dangerous factionalism of Song politics. However, as we can see from the example of literati such as Sima Guang (see Chapter Three), there was always an ambivalence about eremitic withdrawal: was it really the right thing to do, or did the literatus always have the obligation to serve the state, even at personal risk?

In the Yuan, by contrast, the situation was radically different. The efficient and highly mobile Mongol armies had swept out of central and inner Asia into north China, where they had rapidly overcome the Jurchen Jin dynasty who had replaced the Northern Song. The Mongols then continued, with more difficulty in unfamiliar terrain, to conquer the Southern Song, which they accomplished by 1279. For just

under a century, until 1368, they ruled all of China, the first non-Han ethnic group ever to control the whole Chinese landmass. This was a dreadful shock to the Chinese system; the literati saw their role as the governing elite and the arbiters of culture threatened by alien rule.

Many Chinese literati families refused to take office under the conquering dynasty, even when it had become well-established and its authority was not seriously disputed. At the same time, the Mongol rulers distrusted the Chinese, whose ways were so different from their own, especially the southern Chinese (now the majority of the population), who had not had time to grow accustomed to non-Han rule as those in the north had. The Yuan rulers preferred to employ as senior officials members of other ethnic groups such as Uyghurs or Khitans. This situation meant that the Chinese elite need have no hesitation—indeed they might have no choice—about withdrawing from government into private life, and pursuing a life of leisure in a garden environment. The neo-Confucian ideology which had developed in the Song placed a very high value on the virtues of loyalty (for men) and chastity (for women; i.e. lifelong fidelity to a deceased husband), thus providing a moral underpinning to the refusal to take office, out of loyalty to the defeated Song dynasty.

The political situation also meant that, deprived of the traditional career path and the necessity of studying the classics in preparation for the government examinations, the erstwhile scholar-official class was compelled or attracted towards other ways of making a living and other subjects of study. As a result, many literati turned to careers such as medicine, previously regarded as beneath their dignity, so that the social status of doctors and other professionals improved, leading to significant changes in the Chinese social structure.

An important cultural or artistic development related to social change in the Yuan was that landscape became unquestionably the dominant form of painting. In both Northern and Southern Song, landscape painting—usually representing idealized versions of well-known real landscapes—had certainly been an important art-form, but bird-and-flower painting and genre scenes had also been much admired. Now, however, landscape painting gained an unprecedented importance, and it was more closely associated with the personality of the artist than ever before (fig. 68). In the Song, as we saw, Li Gonglin's "Mountain Villa" (see fig. 50 on pages 44 and 45) had been rather exceptional in its presentation of the owner-artist's personal landscape. Now such personalized landscapes, real or imaginary, were to appear much more frequently. One of the reasons for this was that in the early Yuan, there was no court patronage

of painting (though this changed later), so artists turned to painting for each other and for like-minded friends, rather than trying to impress the authorities. All the social and cultural changes outlined here inevitably had an influence on garden culture in the Yuan. Some scholars see the Yuan as a pivotal era in starting a change from gardens as imitations or reproductions of real landscapes to gardens as representations or expressions of ideal landscapes, a change which can be linked to the change in landscape painting from the impersonal and monumental to the personal and expressive. Others, however, would place such a change in garden style later in the Ming.

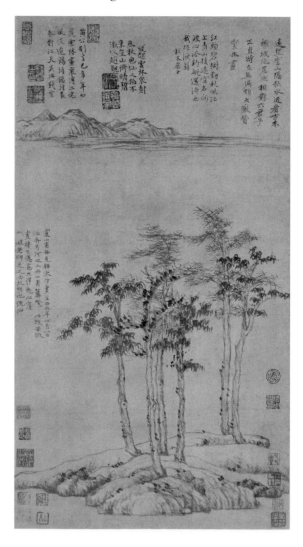

Fig. 68 *Six Gentlemen* (1345)
Ni Zan (1301–1374)
Hanging scroll, ink on paper
Height 61.9 cm, width 33.3 cm
Shanghai Museum

The "six gentlemen" of the title are the craggy old pine trees, upright and strong against wind and weather, representing the endurance of China's culture under Mongol rule. The apparent simplicity, spare composition, and extensive empty spaces of Ni's paintings are understood to represent his sense of desolation and withdrawal from the world.

Family Landscapes

Detailed records of private gardens in the Yuan are rather sparse, though decorative arts can give us some idea of how they were conceptualized and what they might contain (fig. 69).

Some of the culture surrounding gardens as eremitic retreats in the Yuan dynasty can be recovered from a web of familial and friendship connections centered on the city of Wuxing (today's Huzhou, in the northern part of Zhejiang Province, just south of Lake Tai). This was the home of the painter and calligrapher Zhao Mengfu (1254–1322) and his wife Guan Daosheng (1262–1319), also an artist; she was particularly celebrated for her paintings of bamboo (fig. 70). Zhao Mengfu, a descendant of the Song imperial family, owned several properties in Wuxing including half of his father's splendid chrysanthemum garden, all remnants of an estate granted to his great-great-grandfather in the 1160s. Despite

Fig. 69 Plate with carp (mid-14ᵗʰ century)
Diameter 45.7 cm
Metropolitan Museum of Art, New York

The center of this Yuan-dynasty plate shows a carp in a pond among reeds, water-chestnuts, and duckweed, perhaps to be understood as shorthand for a garden scene. The rim shows a stylized floral diaper pattern while the cavetto (the curved part between rim and base) is decorated with chrysanthemum scrolls, chrysanthemums being a favorite garden flower. The blue-and-white porcelain ware which we think of as characteristic of the Yuan and Ming dynasties came into existence at this time partly because the extent of the Mongol empire made it practical for cobalt, an essential ingredient for the blue pigment, to be imported from Persia (Iran), while much blue-and-white ware was produced for export from China to central and western Asia.

Fig. 70 *Bamboo Groves in Mist and Rain* (1308; detail)
Guan Daosheng
Ink on paper
Dimensions of the complete scroll: height 23.1 cm, length 113.7 cm
Palace Museum, Taibei

Guan Daosheng is considered to be China's greatest female visual artist. She specialized in the painting of bamboo, particularly associated with the literati because of its close relationship to calligraphy. Guan Daosheng established bamboo as a typical subject for later women painters (see fig. 127 on page 108).

his imperial lineage, Zhao nevertheless served the Yuan dynasty in both north and south China. In his native city, he constructed a garden named Lotus Blossom Manor (*Lianhua zhuang*). As his studio he used a building named Gull Wave Pavilion (*Oubo ting*), which enjoyed a view towards the Bian mountains just north-west of Wuxing. These mountains had a long-standing reputation as a refuge and retreat. The allusion to seagulls or terns in the pavilion name comes from the Daoist classic *Liezi*: the wild gulls will not flee but will flock to the man who is truly at one

with the cosmos (this becomes a common trope in later gardens). Daoism, with its message of self-cultivation and non-action, had a powerful hold over the elite in the Yuan period, even those who, like Zhao, followed a Confucian official career and adhered to neo-Confucian philosophical ideals.

One of Zhao's most famous paintings is *Autumn Colors on the Qiao and Hua Mountains*, which he painted after returning from Beijing to the south in 1295 (fig. 71). The two mountains referred to are near Ji'nan in Shandong, where Zhao served as an official

Fig. 71 *Autumn Colors on the Qiao and Hua Mountains* (1295)

Zhao Mengfu
Handscroll, ink and color on paper
Height 28.4 cm, length 93.2 cm
Palace Museum, Taibei

Zhao Mengfu created this painting for his friend Zhou Mi in a deliberately archaic style recalling the olden days when Zhou's ancestors had lived in the region of these mountains, which do actually have the contrasting shapes depicted by Zhao.

Fig. 72 *Twin Pines, Level Distance*

Zhao Mengfu
Handscroll, ink on paper
Height 26.8 cm, length 107.5 cm
Metropolitan Museum of Art, New York

This painting represents a radical new departure in art: Zhao has developed a new style of landscape ("a bit different," as he says in his inscription on the painting), abandoning realism in favor of calligraphic brushwork expressing personal emotion and identity. In Chinese culture, the pine tree is a symbol of endurance, and these twin pines perhaps represent—for both Zhao and Dong Yeyun, the friend for whom he created the painting—their own survival under Mongol rule, and the endurance of China's culture.

from 1292 to 1295; he then spent a short period in Beijing before returning south. The artist's own inscription on the painting explains that he painted it for his friend Zhou Mi (1232–1298), whose family originated from Shandong. The family had moved south after the conquest of north China by the Jin dynasty in 1126, so Zhou Mi had never known the land of his ancestors, and lived in Wuxing, calling himself "the Old Man from the South Side of the Bian Mountains," until he moved to Hangzhou after the Mongol conquest of the south. Zhou was a fervent Song loyalist

and never took office under the Yuan. The two men therefore had very different views of how to accommodate the political situation: Zhou believed that loyalty to the Song required him to go into retirement, while Zhao felt that duty called him to office in order to mitigate the faults of the new regime (fig. 72). Zhao's painting for Zhou Mi is an example of a new engagement in Yuan-dynasty art with the landscape as an expression of personal association and ownership.

Some years later, in 1302, Zhao painted a handscroll titled *Water Village* for another friend,

Qian Zhongding, while visiting him in his retirement in the Jiangnan area (fig. 73). This is an imaginary landscape, but represents an idealized version of Qian's place of retirement and perhaps also Zhao's ideal for his own retirement: at the time, he was still employed by the Yuan government, but in what was more or less a sinecure.

Towards the end of the Yuan period, Zhao Mengfu's grandson Wang Meng (1308–1385), one of the "Four Great Masters of the Yuan,"[9] created two images of a landscape which was particularly associated with the recipients of these paintings. One was a handscroll (of uncertain date, possibly the 1350s) painted for his cousin's son Cui Sheng, also known as Cui Yanhui; the painting was entitled *The Humble Hermit of the Cloudy Forest*, a name which Cui applied to himself (fig. 74). "Humble Hermit" alludes to the idea promoted by the Tang poet Bai Juyi (see Chapter Two) of the great hermit who can attain withdrawal from the

Fig. 73 *Water Village* (1302)
Zhao Mengfu
Handscroll, ink on paper
Height 24.9 cm, length 120.5 cm
Palace Museum, Beijing

"Water village" is a term often applied to the country towns of the Jiangnan region, set alongside its plentiful canals and rivers. The cottage in which Zhao envisages his friend spending his retirement can be seen in the middle distance of the painting.

Fig. 74 *The Humble Hermit of the Cloudy Forest*
Wang Meng
Handscroll, ink on paper

Wang Meng depicts his relative's place of seclusion in the Bian mountains as a dense forest surrounding a calm lake. Although Cui Sheng had studied in a government college, even before moving to the mountains he never held an official post. He seems to have made a living from calligraphy commissions and by collecting and selling medicinal herbs, becoming one of those literati who turned to commercial or professional activity in place of official service under the restrictions imposed by the Mongol rulers.

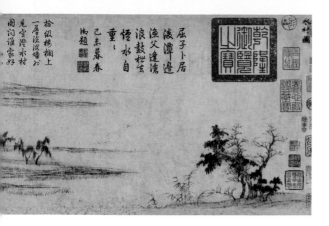

world even at the center of political power, the middling hermit—like Bai himself—who can seclude himself in the city, and the humble or lesser hermit—as Cui styled himself—who withdraws to live in the wilds. The Cui family, who came from Hangzhou, had links of friendship and marriage with the Zhao family extending over several generations.

From a comment on the painting written by a contemporary, we learn that Cui Sheng had become disgusted with the hustle and bustle of the great city of Hangzhou, and was very taken by the tranquility and seclusion of the Bian mountains while he was on a visit to the Zhaos. He therefore decided to settle with his family in the "cloudy forest" and gave himself this new name, marking a new sense of his own identity. The naming of the painting after the cognomen or studio name which Cui applied to himself is a new phenomenon and foreshadows the popularity in the Ming of "cognomen pictures" (*biehao tu*) which represent the recipient's studio name in the form of a garden dwelling (see Chapter Five).

The hanging scroll of 1366 titled *Dwelling in Retreat in the Blue Bian Mountains* (fig. 75)

Fig. 75 *Dwelling in Retreat in the Blue Bian Mountains* (1366)
Wang Meng
Hanging scroll, ink on paper
Height 140.6 cm, width 42.2 cm
Shanghai Museum

Contrasting with the peaceful scene depicted in the earlier *Humble Hermit of the Cloudy Forest* (fig. 74), the towering, distorted forms of the mountains in this painting, one of Wang Meng's greatest creations, suggest that not even a refuge in the mountains can avoid the political and social instability two years before the Yuan dynasty's final collapse.

was painted for another relative, his cousin Zhao Lin (fl. 1350–1370). Zhao served as an official of the Yuan government and was known as a writer and artist, though not of the stature of his grandfather or cousin. He had inherited Zhao Mengfu's Gull Wave Pavilion, with its view of the Bian mountains. The studio and its surroundings seem to have fallen into disrepair while he was away from Wuxing, perhaps owing to local military disturbances linked to the dynastic transition. These disturbances, particularly the conflict between Zhu Yuanzhang (1328–1398), the eventual victor and founder of the Ming, and his rival rebel leader Zhang Shicheng (1321–1367), had been on-going since the 1350s, and by 1366, civil war had overtaken the formerly tranquil area of Wuxing. Wang Meng himself had served the Yuan as an official, but retired amid the instability towards the end of the dynasty, and then moved from his retreat near Hangzhou to Suzhou. It is possible that Wang joined Zhang Shicheng's regime in Suzhou at a time when Zhang was nominally allied with the Yuan central government.

In the mid-1360s, Wang painted a number of such landscapes on the theme of eremitism for various friends, including the impressive *Lofty Recluse in Summer Mountains* for a recipient named as "Recluse Yanming" in Suzhou (figs. 76 and 77). At this time Wang

Figs. 76 and 77   *Lofty Recluse in Summer Mountains* (1365)

Wang Meng
Hanging scroll, ink and color on silk
Height 149 cm, width 63.5 cm
Palace Museum, Beijing

In this detail (left) of Wang Meng's elaborate painting (above), we can see an idealized version of the garden surroundings of Recluse Yanming's retreat, with water, rocks, and trees. Yanming, reclining on a day-bed, is watching a young servant encouraging a pet crane to dance in the open space in front of the building, while an older servant is delivering something on a tray: probably food, as there is a very excited dog just behind him.

was clearly very concerned with questions of social engagement versus reclusion and with familial and cultural continuity in a chaotic time, suggested by the contorted, unstable forms of the landscape in the 1366 painting of the Bian mountains which Zhao Mengfu had once described in verse as a remote and peaceful retreat. This depiction is very different from the calm, open landscape of the "Cloudy Forest" handscroll.

This group of paintings by members of the related Zhao and Wang families illuminates the importance in the Yuan of concepts of eremitism as a response to political events, and the close connection between the choice of going into reclusion and the selection of a location with deep personal meaning in which to enjoy the hermit's life in a garden residence. The identification of place and person shown in a name such as "Humble Hermit of the Cloudy Forest" points to a new sense of interconnection between literatus and landscape/garden, which we will find further developed in the literati gardens of the Ming and Qing.

Imperial Gardens of the Jin and Yuan

There was a variety of different types of garden in the Yuan period, but it is not clear to what extent there was an actual variation in style between them. We can assume that the imperial gardens were more grandiose and splendid than privately owned gardens or the gardens of institutions such as academies and temples. When Khubilai Khan (1162–1227) established the seat of Yuan-dynasty China at his "great capital" Dadu (known to the Mongols as Khanbaliq; roughly the site of later Beijing), some former Jin-dynasty imperial gardens became the basis for those of the Yuan (fig. 78). In turn, the Yuan imperial gardens provided the foundations for the development of the Ming and then the Qing imperial parks and gardens.

As the Jin dynasty, preceding the Yuan, had consolidated their power in northern

Fig. 78 Map of Yuan-dynasty Dadu and surroundings (adapted from Zhou Weiquan's *China Classical Garden History*)

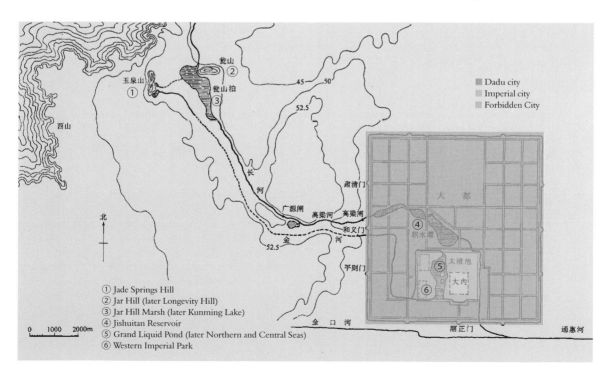

① Jade Springs Hill
② Jar Hill (later Longevity Hill)
③ Jar Hill Marsh (later Kunming Lake)
④ Jishuitan Reservoir
⑤ Grand Liquid Pond (later Northern and Central Seas)
⑥ Western Imperial Park

China, they had moved their capital in 1151 from their "upper capital" (Shangjing), near present-day Harbin in Heilongjiang Province, south to Yanjing, the former "southern capital" of the Khitan Liao dynasty (916–1125), and renamed it the "Central Capital" (Zhongdu). This was located in the south-western part of present-day Beijing. The Jin emperors developed a large number of gardens, parks, and "traveling palaces" in and around the city, and also in more

Fig. 79   In the Jin and Yuan dynasties, Qionghua Island in what is now Beihai Park was smaller than it became in later developments of the imperial park. The Daoist-inspired Palace of Broad Chill on its summit, originally constructed in the Jin dynasty, was replaced in the Qing dynasty by the conspicuous Buddhist dagoba or stupa.

distant parts. The most important of these parks, in the light of later developments in the Yuan, Ming, and Qing, was the Palace of Great Tranquility (*Daning gong*) to the north-east of Zhongdu, where there had previously been a Liao-dynasty "traveling palace." Construction of the park started in 1179, involving the excavation of an existing marshy area to form a lake with a large island (now Qionghua Island) surmounted by a building named Palace of Broad Chill (*Guanghan dian*) after a legendary palace on the moon (fig. 79). The design of the park was influenced by the gardens of the former Song capital Kaifeng, and supposedly some

Fig. 80   *Khubilai Khan Hunting* (1280)
Liu Guandao (c. 1258–1336)
Hanging scroll, ink and color on silk
Height 182.9 cm, width 104.1 cm
Palace Museum, Taibei

After conquering China the Mongol rulers continued some of their traditional pastimes, such as hunting on the grasslands around their old capital Shangdu. In this very un-Chinese landscape painted by a court artist, we see Khubilai Khan (in a splendid ermine coat) with his empress, accompanied by a hunting party. The mounted archer on the left is taking aim at two wild geese; other riders have a gyrfalcon, a hawk, and a cheetah. A caravan of camels is passing in the distance.

Fig. 81 *A Han Dynasty Palace Garden*

Li Rongjin (fl. late 13th–early 14th centuries)
Hanging scroll, ink and color on silk
Height 156.6 cm, width 108.7 cm
Palace Museum, Taibei

Little is known of Li Rongjin, who signed this painting; he is said to have been a student of Wang Zhenpeng (see fig. 59 on page 53), so he was evidently a Yuan court artist. Although the painting represents a fantasy Han palace, it gives us an idea of what the Yuan imperial family might have aimed at in creating their own palace and its gardens.

of the rocks from the North-East Marchmount itself (see Chapter Three) were transported north for use here. Another important Jin imperial park was on Jade Springs Hill (*Yuquan shan*) to the north-west of the capital, previously another Liao "traveling palace." Water from the five springs on this hill fed into the water supply for the Palace of Great Tranquility. Jade Springs Hill was particularly favored by the Jin Emperor Zhangzong (r. 1190–1208) as a summer retreat for hunting.

Once the Mongol rulers of the Yuan dynasty had conquered the Jin in 1215, they moved their capital from Shangdu (known to Europeans as Xanadu, and located south of present-day Xilinhot city in Inner Mongolia) to the site of the Jin capital, though they continued to spend summers in the Shangdu area (fig. 80). Zhongdu had

suffered great damage during the conquest, but the Palace of Great Tranquility had been largely untouched. The Mongols constructed their new capital, which they named Dadu or Great Capital, around the Palace of Great Tranquility (fig. 81). The lake was now named Grand Liquid Pool (*Taiye chi*) and its island the Hill of Myriad Years (*Wansui shan*); they were incorporated into the imperial city to become the basis of the main palace park

(see fig. 78 on page 67). The Grand Liquid Pool covered approximately the area of the Northern Sea (*Beihai*) and Central Sea (*Zhonghai*; now part of Zhongnanhai) in present-day Beijing. The island, probably smaller than the present Qionghua Island, was largely constructed of the fine rocks brought there in Jin times, planted with shady pines and cypresses, with the Palace of Broad Chill at its summit as the main building, and other smaller buildings scattered around its slopes, including a bath-house. Where the water supply from the imperial city moat entered the lake, a water-wheel or pump raised water to the summit of the island, from where it flowed down in two streams and back into the lake. This shows the sophistication of hydraulic engineering at the time; large-scale works had been undertaken to ensure an adequate water supply for the palace and park from Jade Springs Hill, and a separate supply for Dadu city and the city moat from the north-west via Jar Hill Marsh and the city reservoir.

When the palace moat was excavated, the spoil was used to construct a hill (Scenic Hill or *Jingshan*) in the Numinous Park (*Lingyou*), named for King Wen's legendary park (see Chapter One) and situated to the north of the Forbidden City; the park also included a menagerie with "strange beasts and rare birds" for the amusement and interest of the imperial family. Scenic Hill (fig. 82) was located north of the palace probably for *fengshui* reasons, to protect the palace and its inhabitants from dangerous influences from the north. This suggests that the Mongol rulers had already internalized some Chinese cultural concepts, since one would not expect them to regard their own homeland in the north as a source of danger.

The lake known as Jar Hill Marsh to the

Fig. 82   The present-day Jingshan Park in Beijing, across the road from the north gate of the Forbidden City, is based on the artificial hill created in the Yuan dynasty after excavation of the new palace moat.

north-west of Dadu, which was developed in the Yuan as a reservoir for the city, was the origin of what is now Kunming Lake in the Summer Palace (*Yihe yuan*), though it was then much smaller in extent. In the 12th century, the first emperor of the Jin dynasty had constructed a "traveling palace" there, presumably as a hunting lodge: the area was sufficiently far away from the city that it was completely rural.

In 1329, Tugh Temür (Emperor Wenzong of Yuan, 1304–1332, r. 1328–1332), who used the area for fishing and other recreations, ordered the establishment of a Buddhist monastery on the north shore of the lake, which provided the basis for much monastic development in the late imperial period.

Monastic Gardens—the Lion Grove

Both Buddhism and Daoism flourished in the atmosphere of religious tolerance under the Yuan, and monastic or temple gardens seem to have been a prominent garden type. Probably the most widely known garden of the Yuan dynasty is the Lion Grove (*Shizilin*) in Suzhou, which is particularly noted for its rockery (fig. 83). The garden as it is now probably bears little resemblance to its Yuan-dynasty form. It was extensively reconstructed between 1917 and 1925 by its then owners, the Bei family (the family of the Chinese-American architect I. M. Pei), though the rockwork largely retained its late Qing dynasty form, probably similar to that seen in a woodblock-printed illustration from the time of a visit by the Qing Qianlong Emperor (1711–1799, r. 1735–1796) in the 18th century (fig. 84).

The site had been the garden of a scholar-official family in the Song dynasty, but there is no evidence of significant rockwork in the Song garden. In the early 14th century, the garden was occupied by a Zen

Fig. 83   Lion Grove, Suzhou, Jiangsu Province

Buddhist master, Tianru Weize (1286–1354), who appears to have been living there by 1326, when the rocks were already installed. Other evidence, including an account of the monastery written in 1354, suggests that the monastery itself was constructed in 1342 on the initiative of Master Weize's disciples. Weize himself was noted as a poet, and had many interactions with Suzhou literati.

The monastery, which gave its name to the garden, was known as the Lion Grove Monastery of the True Sect of Enlightenment (*Shilin puti zhengzong si*). The description as a "grove" is often applied to Buddhist monasteries, while the "lion" also has associations with Buddhism: it is ridden by the Bodhisattva Manjusri, and the "lion's roar" is a metaphor for the power of Buddhist preaching. Additionally, according to the 1354 account, Master Weize had been ordained by a Zen master at Lion Cliff on Tianmu mountain in Zhejiang, a famous Buddhist site. The name also derived from a rock in the garden shaped like a *suanni*, a mythical beast similar to a lion, so altogether the lion reference had a threefold meaning. By the 16th century the garden had been abandoned, so the lion-shaped rockery formations now to be seen in the garden must be later creations. Indeed, although the original rockwork was much admired at the time, by the 18th century the garden connoisseur Shen Fu (1763–c. 1810) could say that, "It looks more like

Fig. 84   Illustration of Lion Grove from *Nanxun Shengdian* (1771)

The *Glorious Celebration of the Southern Imperial Progress* (*Nanxun Shengdian*) is an illustrated record of a journey to south-east China undertaken in 1771 by the Qianlong Emperor. It includes depictions of many famous gardens of the time, which were often used as lodgings for the imperial party.

a pile of coal dust covered with moss and ant hills, without the least suggestion of the atmosphere of mountains and forests."[10]

The tradition that the garden was designed by the artist Ni Zan (1301–1374; see fig. 68 on page 60) has very little supporting evidence, other than his acquaintance with Master Weize; it is possible that he was one of a group of Suzhou literati with whom Weize consulted about the creation of the garden. A famous painting of the garden attributed to Ni Zan, dated 1372, if it is by Ni Zan or a copy of his work, is more likely to represent the "spirit" or "intention" of the garden than its actuality. An album by the 14th-century painter Xu Ben depicting different scenes or sites in the garden is also idealized but may give more of a sense of the garden's variety; it includes a representation of the rock in the shape of the mythical *suanni*, labelled as "Lion Peak" (fig. 85). Literary records are a more reliable source of information on the early form of the Lion Grove garden: they are quite consistent, indicating that in 1347 it had about twenty buildings and a large expanse of bamboo, in 1350 it had an area of 10 *mu* (0.66 ha) and fewer than twenty buildings, while in 1371 an early Ming writer described it as being small in size, abundant in "strange rocks," with beautiful bamboo groves (Xu Ben's album includes a "Bamboo Valley").

Fig. 85 *Lion Peak* Leaf from the album *Paintings of the Lion Grove*

Xu Ben (14th century)
Ink on paper
Height 22.5 cm, width 27.1 cm
Palace Museum, Taibei

This painting of the Lion Peak (the name is inscribed on the single, standing rock) is one of twelve leaves in the album. Although the paintings probably represent real sites in the garden (all are named), they are certainly idealized. Xu Ben was born in the late Yuan and lived in Suzhou before becoming an official of the newly established Ming government in 1374, so he must have become familiar with the garden not more than thirty years after its creation.

Academy Gardens—Attachment to the Past

Another type of institutional garden in the Yuan was the academy garden. Even after the Mongol conquest, many Song academies (see Chapter Three) were restored, and new academies were established. These provided the Chinese literati, especially those unable or unwilling to hold official positions, with sites where they could engage in intellectual pursuits with like-minded peers. In Yuan writings about academies, landscape was often treated as a repository of Chinese cultural memory. Carrying on the Southern Song practice of founding academies at sites linked to earlier scholars, many Yuan academies were established on sites associated with notable figures of the Song dynasty, indicating a pride in local history and a desire to maintain connections with the Chinese past.

Jiaxuan Academy in Shangrao (in the north-eastern part of today's Jiangxi Province)

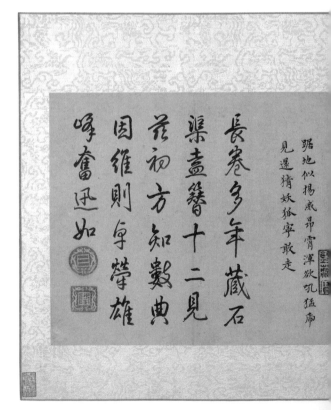

was established on the site where the great poet and Song irredentist Xin Qiji (1140–1207) had retired to farm. The academy's grounds followed the topography of Xin's farm, and indeed "Farming Pavilion" (*Jiaxuan*) was the name of a building originally put up by Xin. A Confucian school was founded there in 1274 (shortly before the fall of south China to the Mongols), renamed Jiaxuan in 1298, and renovated in 1303. An old well and a fishpond which had existed in Xin's time were restored to use as a water supply and reservoir.

Another example is the Stone Gate Grotto (*Shimen dong*) Academy, established in 1294 at a site visited by the 4th–5th century landscape poet Xie Lingyun (see Chapter Two) on his journey into internal exile in Yongjia (today's Wenzhou, in the far south of Zhejiang Province). A commemorative inscription for the foundation emphasizes Xie Lingyun's interest in the landscape: by "wander[ing] and explor[ing] in the mountains," he "comprehended the principles of humanity

and knowledge".[11] In 1336 an official visited Stone Gate Grotto Academy and found it in disrepair, so he allocated funds to rebuild it. The inscription recording this rebuilding reflects the importance to learning of the landscape and the scholarly community: "The academy depends on the flourishing of lofty forests and snowy cascades, and so we have renewed its beauty"; "In seeking humanity and virtue, [scholars] must always have [the opportunity for] lecturing and practice, and what more do they need than the special perspective provided by the mountains and waters?"[12] As in the Song dynasty, the observation of natural phenomena, within the structure of an institutional environment, is emphasized as a route to wisdom. The spirit of Xie Lingyun was certainly an appropriate inspiration for an institution in which philosophical truths would be revealed through the power of landscape.

The Sleeping Dragon Academy (*Longmian shuyuan*) was constructed in 1330 on the site of Li Gonglin's Mountain Villa of that name (see Chapter Three), which had previously been destroyed, presumably to re-use its building materials, by monks from a local Zen monastery. The Chinese scholar who wrote the commemorative inscription described the educated Mongol official who set up the academy as an exemplary Confucian official promoting education; such foundations, therefore, did not always represent opposition or resistance to Mongol rule. Academy foundation narratives often tell of an official coming on a scenic spot associated with a significant historical figure, and being inspired by the landscape to found or renovate an academy, as a means to cultivate more worthy and talented officials for recruitment to office, so again, they were not all intended as a way of avoiding service to the Yuan government, but rather as a way of commemorating the past while adapting to present circumstances.

PART II
GARDENS OF THE LATE IMPERIAL PERIOD—MING DYNASTY

With the Ming dynasty, which replaced the Mongol Yuan in 1368, we enter on what modern historians have designated the "late imperial" period, comprising the Ming and Qing dynasties. These two dynasties, despite some significant differences between them, are felt to represent a political, social, and economic structure quite distinct from what went before, with the relatively brief Yuan dynasty as a transition period foreshadowing some new developments, such as the emphasis on gardens as sites of reclusion and of self-representation.

As China was drawn into the system of globalized trade which developed from the 15th century onwards, economic expansion led to an increase in disposable income for the elite, and the rise of a leisure class who had time and money to expend on such luxuries as the development of elegant gardens. A publishing boom in the mid- to late Ming means that a great quantity of writing survives from the time, giving us an unprecedented insight into what the literate people of the Ming—mostly men, but women too—observed and thought about the topic of gardens. For the first time we are able to obtain a real sense of how gardens were designed, used, and enjoyed by a wide range of people, including literati, women, merchants, and the artisans who created the gardens.

Fig. 86 Please refer to fig. 118 on pages 100 and 101.

CHAPTER FIVE
THE ZENITH OF THE LITERATI GARDEN

After the conquest of China by the forces of rural rebel leader Zhu Yuanzhang (r. 1368–1398) at the end of the Yuan dynasty, and the restoration of Han-Chinese rule under Zhu's Ming dynasty, the position of the literati—largely sidelined from government under the Mongols—did not immediately see great improvement. Zhu Yuanzhang himself, a highly intelligent and capable ruler from a humble background, was very distrustful of the educated elite, and particularly of those from the Suzhou area (the cultural heart of Jiangnan), where support for a rival rebel leader had been strong. Nevertheless, he recognized the need for educated officials, and the literati or scholar-official class soon regained their cultural and political dominance.

From at least the 16th century, as the economy expanded, society became more competitive: increasing access to education—a result of economic growth giving more families the means to pay for tuition and of the publishing boom which led to greater availability of texts and aids to study—meant that the proportion of examination candidates who were able to pass and obtain one of the static number of official posts became smaller and smaller. Economic growth also meant that the expanding class of wealthy merchants, who could afford to acquire the trappings of a cultured lifestyle and to educate their sons to compete for official success, posed a challenge not just to the economic status of the established scholar-official families but to their cultural supremacy. Gardens became one of the battlefields on which the struggle for social success was played out.

Literati gardens of Jiangnan in the late imperial period (the Ming and Qing dynasties), or "scholar gardens" as they are often known, are the gardens which most often come to mind when the phrases

Fig. 87   This pavilion over water is part of the "Jiangnan-style" garden laid out in the Kowloon Walled City Park. The motivation for building a Jiangnan-style garden rather than one in the Cantonese or Lingnan style indigenous to the region is not clear.

Fig. 88 The name of the Lan Su Chinese Garden in Portland, Oregon, combines one of the characters in the Chinese name for Portland with the Su of Suzhou, Portland's sister city. It was constructed in 1999–2000 by a team of Suzhou's famous garden craftsmen, and is intended to reflect the heritage of the substantial Chinese community in Portland, on the Pacific coast, although most of them probably originate from the south of China rather than the Jiangnan region. (photo by author)

"Chinese gardens" or "classical gardens of China" are used. Though by no means the only type or regional form of garden in the late imperial period, these are the gardens which—at least in their late-Qing form—are reproduced in modern versions of "the Chinese garden" recreated either within China or overseas. One example is the garden built on the site of the Kowloon Walled City in Hong Kong after the demolition in the 1990s of the unsafe buildings which had been constructed on the unregulated site from the 1940s onwards (fig. 87). Overseas examples include the Sun Yat-sen Garden in Vancouver and the Lan Su Chinese Garden in Portland, Oregon (fig. 88). The hegemonic status of Jiangnan literati gardens is largely the result of the dominance of elite culture in the late imperial period by the literati of Jiangnan, then and now the most prosperous region of China.

One of the problems about the identification of Jiangnan literati gardens with "the Chinese garden" is that this type of garden is usually presented as an entity that remained basically unchanged over the five and half centuries

of the Ming and Qing dynasties, but it is obviously implausible that any cultural form would stay the same over such a long period of time. On closer examination we can see many changes taking place.

Throughout the late imperial period there is an enormous amount of writing by literati on gardens. Whether describing their own gardens or those of their friends, recording well-known gardens of a particular city or region, inventing imaginary gardens to make up for lack of a real one, creating gardens in fiction (fig. 89), extolling them in poetry, or laying down the law about the proper appreciation of horticultural art, it seems there was scarcely a Ming or Qing literatus who refrained from writing on the topic. However, these writings, though sometimes very detailed, cannot always be relied on to give us a clear picture of how gardens at the time appeared,

Fig. 89 Visitors stroll through the garden of the anti-hero in a woodblock illustration to the 16th-century satirical novel *The Plum in the Golden Vase (Jin Ping Mei)*.

Fig. 90   *Zhi Garden*
(1627)

Zhang Hong (1577–
after 1652)
Album leaf, ink and
color on paper
Height 55 cm, width
55 cm
Los Angeles County
Museum of Art

This is one leaf
of an album, now
divided between two
different collections,
showing views of
a garden called the
Zhi (Stopping)
Garden. The
first leaf shows a
synoptic view of the
whole garden,while
the other leaves,
including this one,
show partial views. We know that the part of the
garden shown here was to the visitor's right on
entering the garden, as the viewpoints from which
the partial views were painted can all be identified
on the first leaf. This was demonstrated by scholarly
work in the 1990s, but it was only in 2010 that a
garden historian in China discovered a text titled
"Record of the Zhi Garden" which revealed the
name of the owner (Wu Liang) and the garden's
location in Changzhou (in present-day Jiangsu
Province). This album provides an unusual visual
record which we can be confident shows the garden
very much as it actually was in the 1620s.

or how they may have changed over time.
We also have a great number of paintings
of gardens, some of which are known to be
real (fig. 90) and some imaginary (though
even the real gardens may not have looked
the way they were painted), as well as many
woodblock prints which may also give us an
idea of how gardens were conceptualized at
the time, while not necessarily representing
any specific garden. We therefore have to be
quite cautious in drawing conclusions about
what gardens were like, either individually or
in general, during the five and a half centuries
of the late imperial era, despite all that the
literati seem to tell us about them.

Elegant versus Vulgar

Research has shown that in the early Ming
dynasty, the Jiangnan literati regarded their
gardens as productive spaces: they were
there to provide fruit, vegetables, and fish
for household consumption and for giving as
gifts to relatives, friends, and acquaintances
(fig. 91). Of course they also provided a
refreshing and relaxing environment for

the owners and their friends and a space in which social activities could take place. However, as the literati felt themselves to be increasingly challenged by the rising merchant class, they needed to assert their cultural authority. One way to do this was to use gardens as markers of their superior "taste," by contrast with the supposed lack of taste shown by "vulgar" members of the merchant class. Since anything to do with production and economic value came to be seen as "vulgar," literati gardens could no longer be acknowledged to be productive but had to be presented as purely esthetic, sites of a high-minded withdrawal from the "dusty world" (fig. 92). That does not, of course, mean that they actually ceased to be productive: they were still producing fruit and vegetables, but that aspect of the garden could hardly be mentioned in the vast corpus of writing on gardens produced by the literati. This change in attitudes seems to have been particularly noticeable in Suzhou, which had recovered from its suppression under the first Ming emperor to become the economic and cultural center of the Jiangnan region, and indeed of the whole country. In other parts of the country, and even in other parts of

Fig. 91 Porcelain dish with underglaze blue decoration of fish and waterweeds (late 16th century)

Diameter 18.4 cm
Metropolitan Museum of Art, New York

The design of fish in a pond suggests the productive use of gardens at this period. A dish like this might have been given to express good wishes: the Chinese word for fish (*yu*) is a homophone of the word for abundance or prosperity, while a pair of fish also symbolizes happy marriage. Gifts of fish from a garden pond would also carry these symbolic meanings.

Fig. 92 *The Studio of True Appreciation* (1549)

Wen Zhengming (1470–1559)
Handscroll, ink and color on paper
Height 36, length 107.8 cm
Shanghai Museum

The great Suzhou literatus and artist Wen Zhengming painted this scroll for the art collector Hua Xia of Wuxi, with whose family he was closely involved. Hua kept his collection in his Studio of True Appreciation (or Connoisseurship—*Zhenshang zhai*). The studio is shown as a simple thatched cottage surrounded by pine trees and Lake Tai rocks in a garden-like rural setting, but it is of course most unlikely that the sharp-witted connoisseur would have entrusted his valuable collection to such an insecure structure. This is a realm of pure imagination to which we can be transported by viewing works of art.

Fig. 93 *South Stream Thatched Hall* (1569; detail)
Wen Boren (1502–1575)
Ink and color on paper
Dimensions of the complete handscroll: height 34.8 cm,
length 713.8 cm
Palace Museum, Beijing

The straightforwardly named South Stream Thatched
Hall (*Nanxi caotang*) was the home in Shanghai of Gu
Ying (fl. 1459–1508). By the mid-16th century the
estate became dilapidated; it was then restored by Gu
Ying's descendant, Gu Tianxi, the dedicatee of this
painting (another source calls him Gu Jiuxi). Painted
to commemorate the restoration, this handscroll
emphasizes the rustic yet elegant simplicity of the
estate and its environment.

Jiangnan, these changes may have come more
slowly, if at all. As we will see in Chapter
Seven, some literati in Zhejiang were happy
to associate their gardens with household
food production.

Another way in which gardens could
provide a site for the literati to display their
superior taste was in the naming of gardens
and garden features. Up to the middle of the
16th century, garden nomenclature is mostly
quite straightforward. Garden residences
often bear names such as "Eastern Garden
of the So-and-So Family," or "South Stream
Thatched Hall" (fig. 93). Names of features
within the garden may indicate some aspect
of the owner's personal interests, perhaps
to do with Confucian or Buddhist ideology,
but usually nothing very obscure. In the
later 16th century, however, and even more
in the 17th century, names become noticeably
more allusive and recherché. They present
a deliberate challenge to the visitor: is he
sufficiently highly educated to decipher

the hidden meaning? Some literati, such as
Xie Zhaozhe (1567–1624), poured scorn
on the use of insufficiently subtle names:
"A waterside enclosure overlooking a pond
is bound to be called 'Sky Light and Cloud
Shadows.' If it is 'Thoughts of Hao and Pu'
you usually see a fishpond."[13] The name
of the river Hao embodies an extremely
recognizable reference to the enjoyment
of fish in the water from the Daoist classic
Zhuangzi. What an unimaginative name for
a pond! And how vulgar to associate the
subtlety of Daoist philosophy with such a
mundane purpose as raising fish for the table!
Another literatus complimented a friend's
good taste by praising the names of his many
garden features "not one of which reveals the

Fig. 94 Woodblock-printed illustration of the
Yushan (Allegory Mountain) Garden created by
Qi Biaojia (1603–1645), drawn in 1638 by Chen
Guoguang and published in Qi's *Notes on Yushan*.
This was the garden admired by Qi's friend Zhang
Dai for its elegance and the absence of vulgarity
in the names of its features (which are marked on
the illustration). Zhang Yifan, a son of the famous
garden designer Zhang Lian (see Chapter Eight), was
involved in the design of the garden.

slightest sign of vulgarity"[14] (fig. 94).

Some literati, on the other hand, resisted such competitive game-playing. The leading 16th-century writer and literary critic Wang Shizhen (1526–1590) made fun of an over-sensitive acquaintance who disliked the name "Crab's Claw" bestowed on a rock of this shape (too obvious), by pretending that it actually referred to an obscure historical anecdote. But Wang Shizhen was a proponent of the "archaistic" (*fugu*) movement in literature, which took Han-dynasty writing as

the model for prose, and the Tang for poetry, so it is perhaps not surprising if he was not at the forefront of garden fashions. His son Wang Shiqi (1554–?) actually drew a parallel between his father's preferences in literary style and in garden design, saying he "equated massive structure with fine workmanship" (fig. 95), contrasting these with his own preference for "spacious expansiveness and naturalness." It is possible, therefore, to link attitudes to garden style with attitudes to other cultural forms.

Fig. 95 *Lesser Jetavana Garden* Leaf from the album *Record of a Journey* (1574)

Qian Gu (1508–1578)
Ink and color on paper
Height 28.5 cm, width 39.1 cm
Palace Museum, Taibei

This shows part of the garden of the writer Wang Shizhen in Taicang, near Suzhou. The painting shows the "massive structure" of the rockery work, designed by the master craftsman Zhang Nanyang (see Chapter Eight). Note also the masonry-faced pond and the extensive cherry-orchard behind the red-painted hall on the left, indicative of conservative tastes in garden style.

The Influence of Landscape Painting

Certainly we can connect changing fashions in the art of landscape painting in the latter part of the 16th century to changing fashions in garden style in the early 17th. Dong Qichang (1555–1636) played the sort of dominant role in art criticism which Wang Shizhen played in the literary field, and Dong's influence has if anything been even more lasting. He responded to the growing sensitivity about "elegance" versus "vulgarity" by redefining the criteria for artistic judgment, drawing a division between "amateur" (gentlemanly) and "professional" (vulgar) artists. He looked back to the landscape art of the "Four Great Masters of the Yuan Dynasty" as the highest form of representational art (calligraphy rather than painting was the highest form of visual art) and the most suitable for the gentleman-amateur painter (fig. 96). The purpose of such art was to express the inner spirit of the artist, not to give an accurate representation of the external world. One of its notable characteristics is a very restricted use of color, whereas earlier in the Ming dynasty, color had been freely used by both professional and amateur (literati) artists, in so far as a clear distinction can actually be made between the two categories. Clearly, this emphasis on restraint and apparent simplicity is related

Fig. 96   *Mist and Clouds on Xishan*
Dong Qichang
Hanging scroll, ink on paper
Height 97.2 cm, width 48.9 cm
Shanghai Museum

This landscape painting follows the style of the Yuan master Ni Zan (see fig. 68 on page 60), much admired by Dong Qichang, with some ink effects borrowed from Huang Gongwang (1269–1354), another Yuan master.

Fig. 97   *Snowy Studio* Leaf from the album *Twelve Views of a Suburban Garden* (1625)

Shen Shichong (fl. 1611–1640)
Ink and color on paper
Height 30.1 cm, width 47.5 cm
Palace Museum, Taibei

This album shows various views of the 17th-century Pleasure in the Suburbs Garden (*Lejiao yuan*) in Taicang, near Suzhou. It belonged to the literatus Wang Shimin (1592–1680) and was designed by Zhang Lian (see Chapter Eight and fig. 137 on page 114). The simple thatched structures, earthen mounds, and sparse trees contrast with the 16th-century garden of Wang Shizhen (see fig. 95 on page 81), who though not a relative was a great friend of Wang Shimin's grandfather.

Fig. 98 The stone columns of the Canglang Pavilion, in the Suzhou garden of that name (see fig. 10 on page 10) bear a couplet reading (on right) "The pure breeze and bright moon are beyond price" and (on left) "The nearby waters and distant mountains all have emotion." Appropriately, the first line is taken from a poem on the garden by the Song poet Ouyang Xiu (1007–1072), while the second comes from a poem on Suzhou by the garden's original owner, Su Shunqin.

Calligraphy and Kunqu Opera

Not only were literati gardens associated with landscape painting, they were also closely connected with other art forms. Gardens had been sites for writing poetry as well as being the subjects of poetry from much earlier in history. Calligraphy—the art form most prized by the literati—played an important role in the garden: the name of the garden set over its entrance appeared in calligraphic form, as did the names of garden features, applied to buildings or carved into rocks. Furthermore, it became fashionable to attach vertical plaques to the pillars on either side of a building's doors, engraved with antithetical couplets relevant to the purpose of the building or its environment, again written in calligraphic form (fig. 98). The owner of the garden might write such calligraphic pieces in his own hand, but he was more likely to invite his friends or acquaintances to do so, especially if any of them were particularly noted calligraphers. He might well also invite such a person to invent as well as inscribe the name of the building or other feature. He would thus accumulate visible evidence of his social network as well as his own and his friends' artistic and literary taste. Zheng Yuanxun (1603/4–1644), a literatus and amateur artist from a merchant background, was proud to record that the name of his garden in Yangzhou, the Garden of Shade (see Chapters Seven and Eight), was bestowed by the great Dong Qichang, who also wrote the name in his prized calligraphy, to be installed above the main gate.

to the wider emphasis in literati esthetics on elegance (*ya*) and blandness (*dan*).

It took a little time for Dong Qichang's ideas on landscape painting to percolate through to the art of garden design, but it seems clear that they did so around the beginning of the 17th century. At this time, evidence from both art and literature indicates that there was a change from a style of garden which incorporated large and imposing rockeries intended to be seen as miniaturized mountains, fairly large, dense plantings of a single type of tree or plant, and rectangular, masonry-faced ponds (as in fig. 95 on page 81), to a simpler, more open layout, in which mountains were suggested by a few rocks or earthen mounds rather than directly represented, the ponds and water-courses appeared more natural and irregular, and the focus was on individual trees and plants or small groups of them (fig. 97). This parallels the change in landscape-painting preferences from the grand, mountainous landscapes of the Northern Song dynasty (see fig. 64 on page 56) to the open composition and restrained, more suggestive style in the work of the Yuan masters (see, for example, fig. 68 on page 60).

Another art form which became particularly closely associated with literati gardens in the late Ming was drama, particularly the elegant, melodious, and highly stylized form of musical theater known today as *kunqu* but in the late imperial period usually called *chuanqi* or "transmission of the strange." There was a positive craze for drama among the late-Ming literati; this is

Fig. 99 Illustration to *Rain on the Wutong Trees*, published by Guqu zhai (Wanli period, 1573–1620)

The Yuan-dynasty drama *Rain on the Wutong Trees* (*Wutong yu*) tells the ever-popular story of the Tang Emperor Xuanzong and his Honored Consort Yang. This illustration, from a Ming-dynasty anthology of Yuan plays, shows Lady Yang dancing in a palace courtyard on a carpet functioning as the stage, for the emperor's entertainment. After her death, the emperor compares the rain dripping from the trees to his own sorrowful tears. The use of the carpet reflects Ming performance practice.

Fig. 100 A 1617 woodblock-printed edition of Tang Xianzu's (1550–1616) drama *The Peony Pavilion*, with illustrations carved by members of the celebrated Huang family of wood engravers. This illustration shows the heroine Du Liniang seated in a room overlooking a garden pond, and dreaming of a romantic encounter beside the eponymous pavilion.

probably related to the interest in individual psychology and authentic personal identity associated with the ideas of the great Ming philosopher Wang Shouren (also known as Wang Yangming, 1472–1529) and his later followers. Many late-Ming literati prided themselves on their ability to write compelling dramas and to appreciate the finer points in the work of others; wealthy families would often keep their own drama troupes of actors and musicians, who would perform for the enjoyment of the household and their friends and relatives, usually

in the family's own garden. In the Ming and early Qing, there was no need for a purpose-built theater: a performance could be put on in any suitable building or open space in the garden which the audience might choose, simply by laying down a red carpet to define

the "stage" area (fig. 99). Thus the garden itself could be used as the setting for the dramatic action. This was particularly apt when the play was actually set in a garden.

With the expansion of publishing in the late Ming, many dramas were printed, often in finely illustrated editions, and read by people who might have little or no opportunity to see the drama being performed (fig. 100). The illustrations to dramas and to works of prose fiction, in which significant events often took place in gardens, no doubt helped to spread ideas of what a garden should look like beyond the south-east of China—where most publishing took place—to other regions, thus probably leading to a more unified style of garden design throughout the country compared to earlier times.

Fig. 101 *The Garden for Seeking My Own Aims* (1564: detail)
Qian Gu
Ink and color on paper
Dimensions of the complete handscroll: height 29.8 cm, length 190.5 cm
Palace Museum, Beijing

Many of the features depicted in this handscroll, such as the trellis fence of roses and roseleaf raspberry (*Rubus rosifolius*) and the study named "Enjoying Friendship" on the left, in which Zhang Fengyi is sitting at a red-lacquered desk, can be identified from the description of the garden written by Zhang's friend Wang Shizhen. This suggests that Qian Gu's painting is a fairly accurate representation of the garden's actual appearance.

The Meaning of Garden Names

A very important aspect of literati gardens, related to their use for social activities intended to enhance the owner's social network and thus promote his official career, was their function as a form of self-representation by the owner. The choice of a name for the garden was not only an indication of the garden owner's "taste" but also a crucial way for him to suggest what his chief interest or priority was. Thus Wang Shizhen, the leading literary critic referred to above, who was a devotee of Buddhism, named part of his garden "Lesser Jetavana" (*Xiao Qiyuan*) after a park in which the historical Buddha preached (the name of the garden itself, the Yanzhou or Yanshan Garden, comes from indigenous mythical geography). His friend Zhang Fengyi (1527–1613), who never served as an official but made a living by writing plays, named his much more modest garden the "Garden for Seeking My Own Aims" (*Qiuzhi yuan*), to indicate that he did not seek grandeur but was content to enjoy a simple life (fig. 101).

The identification of garden with owner is clearly shown in the phenomenon of the "cognomen picture," a genre of painting in which the painter depicts the cognomen or studio name of the recipient in the form of a garden or garden structure, though what is being represented need not be an actually

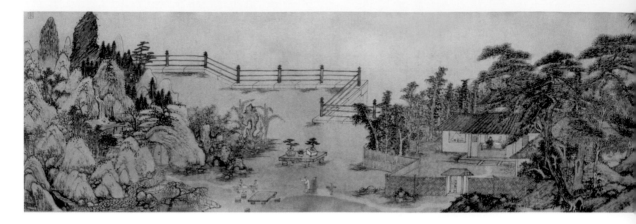

existing garden but rather the personality of the individual (fig. 102). This was a further development of the identification of person with place manifested in representations of eremitic gardens in the Yuan, as discussed in Chapter Four.

The naming of sites within a garden, as opposed to the garden itself, was not entirely under the control of the owner, since it was customary to invite friends and acquaintances to choose at least some names, though presumably the owner could avoid adopting any that he felt to be really inappropriate. We saw that in the Song-dynasty Garden of Solitary Enjoyment the owner Sima Guang named the different sites according to the theme of historical figures whom he particularly admired and wished to emulate (or to be thought to emulate). In the late imperial period, it seems to be less often the case that garden features were named thematically: more usually they were a mixture of the descriptive and the allusive, where the allusions could be to local history and identity, to classical texts, or to the particular interests of the owner.

We can take as an example a late-Ming

Fig. 102 *Friend of the Pines*
Du Qiong (1396–1474)
Handscroll, ink and color on paper
Height 28.8 cm, length 92.5 cm
Palace Museum, Beijing

This is the earliest known example of the Ming genre of "cognomen pictures." In the absence of an inscription, we only know that it is such through a comment by the late-Ming art critic Zhang Chou (1577–1643) who first discussed the genre, telling us that Du painted the image for his brother-in-law Wei Bencheng, whose studio name was "Friend of the Pines" (*Yousong*); otherwise we might think it was simply a painting of a garden. The genre was particularly associated with the Suzhou school of painters in the 15th to 16th centuries, who also produced many topographical paintings of Suzhou's scenery. The name "Friend of the Pines" suggests Wei's self-identification with these evergreen, long-lived trees which flourish among remote mountains.

garden in Beijing (though it was modeled on the gardens of Jiangnan), the Ladle Garden or Dipper Garden (*Shaoyuan*; fig. 103) of the literatus and rock collector Mi Wanzhong (1570–1628), who claimed descent from the Song-dynasty petrophile Mi Fu (see fig. 55 on page 50). The name of the garden suggests a mere ladleful of water, alluding both to its modest size and to its preponderance of water, a rare and valued quality for a garden

in the arid north. The garden contained several features whose names are simply descriptive, such as Meandering Bridge (*Weiyi liang*) for a zigzag bridge across the pond or Crossing of Hewn Trees (*Chaya du*) for a set of "stepping stones" made of old tree-stumps. Perhaps the most practical name is Steaming Clouds (*Zheng yun*), applied to a bath-house! Other names are descriptive at first sight but also embody further allusions, such as Bamboo Foreshore (*Linyu shi*), where the word *linyu*, as a type of bamboo, is taken from a 3rd-century poem "Rhapsody on the Capital of Wu," thus displaying the owner's familiarity with classical literature and also linking this garden in the north to the gardens of the south in the ancient state of Wu (approximately present-day Jiangsu Province). Another example is the name Wind in the Pines and the Moon on Water (literally Pine Wind Water Moon, *Songfeng shuiyue*) applied to a rocky waterside mound planted with pines and junipers: thus it describes the natural phenomena to be heard and seen there, the sound of the pines blown by the wind and the reflection of the moon in the water, but the phrase "water moon" also refers to an aspect of the Bodhisattva Guanyin as the Water-Moon Guanyin, a Buddhist image of the unreality of all phenomena. A further Buddhist image is contained in Bridge of Tasseled Clouds (*Yingyun qiao*) where the phrase "tasseled clouds"—or "clouds the color of tassels," meaning the tassels attached to official hats—comes from a Buddhist text; at the same time it suggests the shape of the

high arched bridge, reminiscent of a rainbow among clouds. But in addition to Buddhism, Mi Wanzhong also incorporated Daoism into his garden, naming a boat-shaped building Supreme Unity Leaf (*Taiyi ye*), Supreme Unity being a Daoist concept and "leaf" suggesting a small boat afloat on the water. Thus Mi Wanzhong as the garden's owner gives us a sense of himself as someone who not only loves nature but has a high degree of traditional learning while also being imbued with both Buddhist and Daoist spirituality.

We can see, therefore, that by the late Ming, the gardens of the educated elite were not just pleasant environments in which they could enjoy relaxing, spending time with friends, or socializing with others who might help to advance their careers in politics or cultural life. Gardens had become sites both for the self-representation of individuals, showing their personal interests and preferences, and for their self-representation as a class, whose dominance of society and culture was already beginning to weaken.

Fig. 103 *The Ladle Garden* (1615; detail)
Wu Bin (1573–1620)
Handscroll, ink and color on paper
Height 30.6 cm, length 288.5 cm
Peking University Library

The Bridge of Tasseled Clouds can be seen on the right of the handscroll, not far in from the entrance to the garden. Wind in the Pines and the Moon on Water is the tree-capped mound visible to the left of the zigzag Meandering Bridge. The bath-house Steaming Clouds is not shown: it is probably concealed among the bamboo behind the two-storey building seen to the right of the tall, thin "bamboo-shoot" rocks.

CHAPTER SIX

IMPERIAL AND ARISTOCRATIC GARDENS OF THE MING

Although the gardens of the Qing emperors have been extensively studied in both China and the West, surprisingly little attention has been paid to imperial gardens of the preceding Ming dynasty. The Ming emperors apparently preferred to remain inside the imperial palace and grounds within the walls of the capital, rather than establishing numerous gardens and parks outside, as the Qing emperors did. The Ming imperial gardens within Beijing were then further developed and reconstructed during the Qing dynasty, so their original form is scarcely perceptible today. As a result the Ming imperial gardens have made less of an impact on popular and scholarly imagination.

The Emperors' Gardens

Despite their relative obscurity, it is possible to recover a good deal of information on the Ming imperial gardens. There is considerable continuity between the layout of the palace grounds from the Yuan dynasty through the Ming to the Qing (and indeed to the present day). During the Ming, there were gardens within the walls of the Forbidden City itself for the day-to-day recreation of the emperor and his women, the main one being on the site of the present Qing "Imperial Flower Garden" (*Yuhuayuan*), in the northernmost part of the Forbidden City (fig. 104). Outside the Forbidden City itself, the Eastern Park

was situated within the south-east corner of the "imperial city," with its eastern margin formed by what is now the street Nanheyan. (The "imperial city" refers to the whole palace complex including the residence of the imperial family—the Forbidden City—and the government offices and other buildings to its south such as the ancestral temple.) There was also the Hill of Myriad Years to the north of the Forbidden City, today's Jingshan Park,

Fig. 104   The main garden within the Ming-dynasty Forbidden City was on the same site, and had much the same layout, as the surviving Qing-dynasty garden. The building shown here is the Pavilion of Ten Thousand Springtimes, located on the east side of the garden. It is symmetrically matched on the west side by the Pavilion of a Thousand Autumns; both were originally constructed in the reign of the Jiajing Emperor (1507–1566). The structure of the pavilions, with their round upper stories surmounting rectangular lower stories, alludes to the traditional cosmological belief that "heaven is round and earth is square."

Fig. 105 *Two Rabbits under a Wutong Tree*
Leng Mei (fl. 1677–1742)
Hanging scroll, ink and color on silk
Height 176.2 cm, width 95 cm
Palace Museum, Beijing

The wutong tree and chrysanthemum flowers
show that the season is autumn: this would be an
appropriate image for display during that season.
The rabbits allude to the practice of eating "heating"
food, according to traditional Chinese medical lore,
in order to counteract the winter cold.

originally created in the Yuan dynasty (see
Chapter Four), and sometimes known as Coal
Hill (*Meishan*). The latter name dates from at
least the Ming: supposedly a stock of coal was
kept buried under the artificial hill in case the
city was besieged. The main imperial pleasure-
ground was the Western Park (*Xiyuan*): this
covered the areas of today's Beihai Park (the
"Northern Sea" or lake) and of Zhongnanhai
("Central and Southern Seas"), which now
houses the highest level of China's central
government. The water-supply for these lakes
and for the Forbidden City entered the imperial

city from the north; during the 16th century,
several shrines to water-gods were built at
the inflow, emphasizing the importance, to
the imperial city and to the capital as a whole,
of this vital source of water for irrigation, fire
prevention, and everyday use.

The Western Park contained a number
of separate garden areas, such as the Pepper
Garden (also called the Banana-Palm Garden:
the pronunciation, *Jiaoyuan*, is the same)
on the eastern bank of the Central Sea, and
the Hare Garden (*Tuyuan*) on the extreme
western edge of the park. The name of the
Hare Garden alludes to a princely garden
or park in the distant historical past, but
the area probably included an actual rabbit
warren: on the Double Ninth Festival in
autumn, when it was customary to climb
to a height, the emperor would ascend the
rockery mountain in the Hare Garden, drink
chrysanthemum wine for long life, and eat
spicy hare or rabbit to ward off the cold of the
approaching winter (fig. 105). To the north of
the Hare Garden was an area where flowers
and fruit were grown for use in the palace.
The Western Park was thus used partly to
produce supplies for the imperial household.
The park also contained a parade ground for
the palace guard, a Buddhist temple complex,
a boat-house for the boats to transport the
emperor and his retinue on the lakes, a
menagerie where wild animals were kept for
the emperor's amusement, and a number of
buildings where the emperor could stay, rest,
eat, or enjoy the view. Some buildings were set
aside for the use of the empress and imperial
consorts, particularly for rituals connected
with silk production, the female equivalent
of the agricultural rituals performed by the
emperor in the southern part of the park.
During his long reign, the Jiajing Emperor
(r. 1522–1566) actually moved out of the
Forbidden City to live in the Western Park,
after a failed assassination attempt against
him in the palace. The park already contained

references to Daoism, for example in the assimilation of islands in the lakes to the islands of the immortals, but the emperor, who was a devout follower of Daoism, renamed many sites with Daoist names, and built a large number of new buildings as sites of Daoist worship and ritual. The emperor spent much of his reign in conflict with his Confucian officials, and despite (or because of) these attempts to assert his identity as a Daoist thearch, many of his new buildings were destroyed after his death.

The gardens within the Forbidden City were, naturally enough, forbidden to anyone but the emperor and his household. From surviving evidence it seems that the main garden, the Imperial Flower Garden, had a mostly rectilinear, axial layout, with rectangular ponds and flower-beds, though in the Wanli reign (1573–1620) a substantial rockery of Lake Tai rocks was added, which included a cave and a waterfall fed by a reservoir at the top of the rockery. Altogether the style of the imperial gardens was probably more conservative than in the case of private gardens. The garden incorporated shrines for Daoist worship: most of the Ming emperors were adherents of Daoist beliefs, though generally less fanatical than the Jiajing Emperor.

Unlike the concealed gardens within the Forbidden City, the imperial parks could be visited by outsiders with special permission from the emperor. In 1413, during the construction of the Ming imperial palace in Beijing (part of the process of moving the capital from Nanjing), the Yongle Emperor (1360–1424, r. 1402–1424) went

to the Eastern Park to watch members of his court playing at "striking the ball and shooting at the willow, allowing the civil and military officials, the ambassadors of the Four Barbarians and the elderly of the capital to participate in the spectatorship."[15] The early Ming emperors would accompany the highest civil and military officials on visits to the Eastern Park as a special honor, and the envoys of tributary states would also be invited to visit it. In this respect it performed a function similar to the Qing imperial park at Chengde (Jehol) where diplomatic envoys were later received, though the Qing arrangements were on a much grander scale (see Chapter Nine).

The Western Park also was sometimes opened to senior officials. For example, in the early summer of 1459, the Emperor Yingzong (r. 1435–1449, 1457–1464) allowed a group of senior officials to tour the park under the guidance of one or more palace eunuchs. Several of the officials left accounts of this mark of imperial favor. These accounts follow what was clearly a standard route through the park, and mostly focus on the buildings they visited, said to be the emperor's favorite spots, though one of the officials, Li Xian (1408–1466), shows much more interest in the flowering plants and trees than the others do.

This practice of granting senior officials a glimpse of the imperial domain continued throughout the Ming, but in the later part of the dynasty it seems to have been less strictly controlled: the socially well-connected Shen Defu (1578–1642), author of *Private Gleanings of the Wanli Era (Wanli yehuo bian)*, a collection of

interesting anecdotes and information from his own time, recalled that as a young man in the capital to take the government examinations in 1619, he went with one of the imperial in-laws to see the menagerie in the Western Park. Perhaps it was only his acquaintance with an imperial relative which got him in there, but he also comments that "enthusiasts" (or "people who like that sort of thing"; he himself found the smell repulsive) would throw chickens or even dogs to the tigers and other animals in their cages; this suggests that a visit was not a particularly rare privilege.

The area to the north-west of Beijing where the Jin and Yuan rulers had had their "traveling palaces" went through considerable transformations from its origins, according to changing imperial needs, though it still remained an important site for the emperors' recreation. The Ming rulers changed the name of the lake from the unappealing Jar Hill Marsh to West Lake, not just because it was to the west of the capital but to recall the beautiful West Lake of Hangzhou in the south. The artist Li Liufang (1575–1629) described the area as "like being in a painting of Jiangnan" (fig. 106). In the early 16th century the hill, then known as Jar Hill (*Wengshan*), had been renamed Gold Hill (*Jinshan*) and the lake became Gold Sea (*Jinhai*). An imperial garden on its shore, unimaginatively named Fine Hill Garden (*Haoshan yuan*), was also known as the Gold Hill Traveling Palace. It was described as being rather plain but with an excellent view from the hill. It seems to have been possible for commoners such as Li Liufang to visit the area, perhaps because

of the large number of Buddhist monasteries which were constructed around the lake in the late Ming and would be open to worshipers.

The Princes' Gardens

A remarkable feature of the organization of the Ming imperial family was the new system inaugurated by the first Ming emperor whereby, on reaching maturity, all the emperor's sons, with the exception of the designated Crown Prince, were dispatched to take up residence in their "fiefdoms" spread across the country. The purpose of this was to avoid conflict in the palace among the potential heirs to the throne and their supporters, since China did not entirely follow the principle of primogeniture and the emperor had the right to appoint as heir the son who he thought would make the best emperor: a sure recipe for endless strife if the sons were not kept apart. These princes and all their descendants were also barred until the very end of the dynasty from any involvement in government; however, they were ritually and socially prominent, and some of them became great patrons of the arts. The princely establishments in different areas would have their own gardens or parks as part of their domains, but their fiefdoms were all outside the economically and politically sensitive Jiangnan area (particularly sensitive at the beginning of the dynasty, when the capital was in Nanjing on the Yangtze). The Jiangnan

Fig. 106 *Landscape*
Li Liufang
Handscroll, ink on paper
Height 29.2 cm, length 347.4 cm
Anhui Provincial Museum

The late-Ming artist Li Liufang failed to pass the government examinations and lived in retirement in Jiading (now within Shanghai Municipality). He painted many landscapes inspired by the scenery of Jiangnan. The lake and hills surrounding the imperial travelling palaces north-west of Beijing could be thought to resemble the Jiangnan landscape.

literati who dominated Ming culture (as we saw in Chapter Five) were therefore mostly unfamiliar with the princely domains and did not write about them, hence the dearth of information on their gardens. Nevertheless, the urban landscapes of the great provincial cities such as Xi'an in Shaanxi or Taiyuan in Shanxi would have been dominated by the princely establishments—as would the rural landscapes around them by princely tomb complexes—in ways quite unfamiliar in Jiangnan.

We can gain a brief glimpse of one palace garden, that of the Prince of Jingjiang (fig. 107), in Guilin, in south-west China, from the account of a Portuguese visitor, Galeote Pereira, who was there around 1550 (though he did not himself see inside): "By report the roofs and towers are glazed green, the greater part of the quadrangle [i.e. the rectangular, walled site of the princely palace] set with savage trees, as oaks, chestnuts, cypress, pine-apples, cedars and other such like that we do want [i.e. lack], in sort that it forms as fresh and singular a wood as can be seen anywhere, wherein are kept stags, gazelles, oxen and cows, and other beasts, for that lord his recreation."[16] Access to such a park or garden was very necessary for the princes, who were not supposed to leave the confines of their city except for certain ritual purposes.

Also in the 16th century, the scholar-official Zhang Han (1511–1593), even though he came from the great southern city of Hangzhou, was greatly impressed by his experience of visiting the palace of the Prince of Qin in Xi'an, as he recalled in a memoir of his posting to Shaanxi:

Whenever visiting the [Prince] of Qin, after the formal banquet in the palace, there was a private banquet in his study, with a chance to enjoy the splendours of the terraces and ponds, the fish and birds. Behind the study canal, water was led in to make two ponds, a great swathe of white lotuses, the ponds stocked with golden fish, and willows growing over it, so that the fish would jump out and would eat titbits thrown for them, making a noise in their struggle for the food. Behind the ponds earth and stones were heaped up into a mountain, with a dozen or so terraces and pavilions on it, where a number of tables would be set up, for the spreading of paintings and histories, and the enjoyment of rare treasures dazzling to the eye. Among the rocks were planted rare flowers and strange trees, the red of the spring crab-apples, the white of the pear blossom, the green of the tender buds, the purple of old *huai* trees, but most outstanding the thousand-branch cypress, its roots and branches convoluted and gnarled in a particularly delightful way. In the rear garden were planted several *mu* of tree peonies, red and purple and pink and white, and among their stunning beauty a heavenly fragrance assailed one. Several tens of peacocks were kept there, flying and calling in their midst, and if one threw them a titbit they would all fly down from the peonies and fight over it, a truly splendid sight.[17]

Fig. 107 Steps of the Chengyun Hall, one of the halls in the palace of the Prince of Jingjiang in Guilin. The marble steps and balustrades are believed to be relics of the original Ming structure, though everything else has been rebuilt. Said to be the best surviving example of a Ming princely palace, the site is now the campus of Guangxi Normal University.

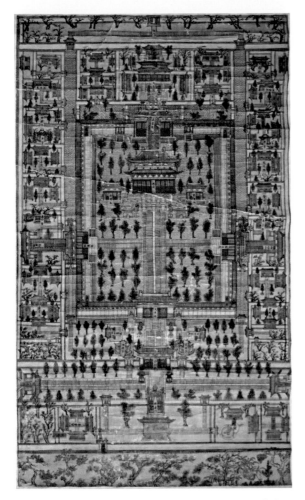

Fig. 108   Ming dynasty map of the Temple of the Veneration of Goodness (*Chongshan si*), Taiyuan, Shanxi Province

This pictorial map of a Buddhist temple originally built in the 1390s by the first Prince of Jin, a son of the Ming founder, clearly shows the density of tree-planting within the extensive temple complex, providing a park-like environment.

The emphasis on water in this and other accounts of Ming princely gardens suggests that the princes had considerable control over water resources in their respective cities, adding to their impact on the urban scene. Their gardens were evidently used as sites of interaction with senior scholar-officials in their regions. The members of princely families, women as well as men, also had an impact on the cityscape through their prominent patronage of Buddhist and Daoist temples. Unlike the princely palaces, such temples were open to all, and their garden-like environment provided a sort of public park for the city inhabitants (fig. 108).

Gardens of the Aristocracy

Although the sons of emperors were removed from the capital, this was not the case for members of the aristocracy (which consisted of ennobled relatives of the emperors' wives and descendants of the founding generals of the dynasty). Thus the city of Nanjing, which was the capital from the founding of the dynasty in 1368 until 1420, had many gardens owned by descendants of the general Xu Da (1332–1385), who was ennobled as Duke of Weiguo for his service in the successful military campaigns waged by the first Ming emperor (fig. 109). In the 16th century, the prominent literatus Wang Shizhen wrote a "Record of Touring the Gardens of Jinling [Nanjing]" explicitly modelled on the Song-dynasty *Record of the Celebrated Gardens of Luoyang*. Of the fifteen gardens which Wang described, ten were owned by members of the Xu

Fig. 109   The Zhan Garden, or Gazing Garden, occupies the site of the original garden of Xu Da, Duke of Weiguo, established in Nanjing in the early Ming dynasty. The garden was given its present name by the Qing Qianlong Emperor when he visited it on one of his southern tours.

family (fig. 110), two by other members of the aristocracy, and only three by literati from scholar-official families. The Jesuit missionary and scholar Matteo Ricci (1552–1610), who was entertained by the tenth Duke of Weiguo in 1599, regarded the Duke's garden as "the most beautiful in the city."

A generation after Wang Shizhen, Gu Qiyuan (1565–1628), who was a native of Nanjing and thus knew the city better than Wang, wrote an update to Wang's "Record," in which he points out that Wang had conflated two gardens, so there were really sixteen in his list; Gu also corrects the locations of some of the gardens, and notes whether they have changed owners or ceased to exist. Of the ten gardens (or eleven by Gu's count) belonging to the Xu family, by Gu's time four had been abandoned (including one site cleared to build a Buddhist monastery), one had been acquired by an official, and one had been divided into three separate gardens belonging to different officials; one of the other aristocratic gardens had also been divided up, but the expression used by Gu implies that it had not been legally purchased but simply taken over by others. Lastly, Gu points out rather disapprovingly that when Wang Shizhen was an official in Nanjing, it would have been possible to visit a number of other gardens, owned by both scholar-officials and aristocrats, but Wang did not do so (or at

least he did not record such visits). It is worth noting here that these aristocratic gardens were evidently "open to the public" to some extent (at least to the right sort of public). Also, while there is plenty of evidence that gardens owned by the literati changed hands frequently, Gu's comments show that this could equally be the case for aristocratic gardens, though from a European perspective we might suppose that the hereditary aristocracy would place a greater value on continuity of ownership, particularly of property granted to them by imperial favor.

Shen Defu, who was a contemporary of Gu Qiyuan, wrote a section in his *Private Gleanings of the Wanli Era* on "Gardens of the Capital" (by this time the capital had long been removed from Nanjing to Beijing); he comments that "the majority of them are the product of the Imperial Relatives, holders of Merit Titles and even wealthy eunuchs".[18] In densely populated Beijing, it was the hereditary aristocracy who had not only the wealth to acquire and maintain extensive gardens but the commitment to the location, whereas most literati—even if some might have been able to come up with the cash—had their roots elsewhere and served only temporarily in the central government, so would be unlikely to invest time and effort, let alone money, in developing gardens there. Even so, Shen's remarks show that most of the notable

aristocratic gardens were located not within the city walls but outside to the north-west, where not only was there more space but there were greater water resources than elsewhere in or around the capital. A 1635 guidebook to Beijing, *Summary of the Sights and Objects of the Imperial Capital (Dijing jingwu lüe)*, records other gardens of the aristocracy in addition to those noted by Shen, and also shows that these gardens could be frequently bought and sold.

It is interesting that Shen Defu attributes the elegant design of a garden belonging to Wan Wei, one of the imperial in-laws, to the influence of his wife, Princess Rui'an, daughter of the Longqing Emperor (1537–1572, r. 1567–1572) and full sister of the Wanli Emperor (1563–1620), so we have an example of a woman taking part in the creation, not

Fig. 110 *The Eastern Garden* (1530)
Wen Zhengming
Handscroll, ink and color on silk
Height 30.2 cm, length 126.4 cm
Palace Museum, Beijing

The Eastern Garden was on a site in Nanjing which had been granted to the Ming general Xu Da. In his day it bore the even more prosaic name of "Garden of the Director of the Imperial Treasury." It was given the name Eastern Garden when it was enlarged by a descendant of Xu Da in the early 16th century, around the time when this handscroll was painted.

Fig. 111 Official portrait of Honored Consort Li, mother of the Wanli Emperor. From a humble family, she entered the household of the Longqing Emperor (at that time the Prince of Yu) as a maidservant at the age of fifteen, and was raised to the rank of Honored Consort after bearing him several children. Her father, Li Wei, was then given the title of Marquis of Wuqing.

just the enjoyment, of a garden. The *Summary of the Sights and Objects of the Imperial Capital* records that in the garden of the Marquis of Wuqing (mentioned by Shen Defu as being under construction in his day) there was a pavilion bearing the name "Pure Elegance" (*Qingya*) in the calligraphy of the Empress Dowager, formerly the Honored Consort Li (1546–1614), the mother of the Wanli Emperor and of Princess Rui'an (fig. 111). Her father, Li Wei, ennobled as the first Marquis of Wuqing, had developed a splendid garden to the north-west of Beijing, bordering on the garden of Mi Wanzhong (see fig. 103 on pages 86 and 87). It was most unusual for women to be publicly acknowledged as having anything to do with the design of a garden or to provide or write the name of a garden feature, so it may be that women of the imperial family were allowed to be exceptional in this as in other ways.

CHAPTER SEVEN
OWNERS AND USERS OF PRIVATE GARDENS

Although literati gardens are the most celebrated type of private (non-imperial) garden in the late-imperial period, they were not the only type of private garden, nor were male literati the only users of their gardens.

The Gardens of Merchants

The gardens of the mercantile class in the late imperial period no doubt have much in common with their gardens in earlier times, as was the case with gardens of the literati, but it is only in the late imperial period that we have enough information to draw any firm conclusions about the nature of merchant gardens.

After the restoration of Han-Chinese rule in 1368 by the Ming dynasty, replacing the Mongol Yuan, a period of social and economic recovery, as we have seen, was followed by substantial economic growth, which really took off in the sixteenth century. At this time China's economy expanded not just because of renewed social stability but also, to a great extent, as a result of the growth in world trade and the influx of South American silver into the world economy following on the age of exploration. One result of this economic expansion was the emergence for the first time of wealthy merchants as a significant social group. To some extent they challenged the literati for influence in society; at the same time, many of them had aspirations for themselves or their descendants to join the educated elite by acquiring education

and familiarity with "high" culture.

By the late imperial period, the Confucian view that merchants occupied the lowest rank of society—if it had ever reflected reality— clearly no longer had any practical application. Merchants operating on both a large and a small scale were essential to the functioning of society in the urbanized, monetized, commoditized economy of the Ming dynasty. Salt- merchants played a particularly important— and lucrative—role in running the state salt monopoly on behalf of the government, which farmed it out to them, while the terms of their licenses also required them to provision the troops stationed on China's northern frontiers to defend them against the incursions of the Mongols and the Manchus. The financial weakness of the state, whose tax-collection methods had not caught up with a decreasingly agrarian and increasingly mercantile economy, led to opportunities for the wealthy to purchase official titles for themselves or their offspring from the government, thus enabling them to move into the official class; mercantile wealth also funded the education of younger family members, enabling them—with talent and luck—to become officials by passing the imperial examinations. Wealthier and better- educated members of the merchant class, therefore, were increasingly hard to distinguish from the literati who had long been recognized as the social elite.

It is not surprising, then, that in the Ming dynasty, particularly in the time of significant

Fig. 112 This view of Hongcun village shows the characteristic Huizhou architecture in its landscape setting. (photo by Lei Gao)

Fig. 113 "Water-mouth" of Hongcun village in the old Huizhou region

The two villages of Hongcun and Xidi have been designated a World Heritage Site since 2000, in recognition of the integration of their vernacular architecture with their water systems in an ecological landscape reflecting the harmony of humankind with nature. Xidi's revival has focused on the development of its water-mouth garden, while in Hongcun there has been a revival of private gardens in a vernacular style. (photo by Lei Gao)

The Huizhou Merchants

economic growth in the mid- to late Ming, merchants began to build substantial gardens which rivaled those of well-off literati. Merchants were able to use their gardens, as the literati did, to hold social events which enabled them to rub shoulders with powerful and influential people. They might also use their gardens as locations for activities such as book publishing, through which they could exert wider cultural influence as well as make money; again, this was something which members of the literati also did. Compared with the literati, however, it was particularly important for merchants to deploy their gardens as a way to raise and consolidate their social status. There is no doubt that the literati felt threatened by rising merchant power and influence. The late-Ming novel of social satire, *The Plum in the Golden Vase* (*Jin Ping Mei*), makes fun of its anti-hero, the wealthy but vulgar merchant Ximen Qing, for his inappropriate social pretensions (see fig. 89 on page 77). When, in Chapter 30, he thinks about buying a new property to which he will add "a reception hall with three bays and an awning in front, a rockery mountain, a flower-garden, a pavilion over the well, an archery hall, a kickball pitch, and other places of entertainment,"[19] this shows his complete failure to understand what a "proper" garden should be like: there is nothing wrong with rockery mountains and well-pavilions, but reception halls should not have awnings, and entertainment facilities such as a kickball pitch are totally out of place.

One region particularly noted for its wealthy merchant families was Huizhou, now known as Shexian (She County), in present-day Anhui Province (fig. 112). This was a mountainous region (it is near the famous scenic mountain Huangshan or Mount Huang) and the cultivable land, though fertile and well-watered, was very limited in area, so merchants from Huizhou had a tradition of traveling to other parts of China, often far from their homes, where they would settle temporarily in order to make money. They came to dominate the salt industry in particular. Some became very wealthy and, as well as educating their sons to become literati, they would use their wealth to acquire social capital through philanthropy, often providing their home regions with paved roads, bridges, temples, and other public works. One distinctive aspect of Huizhou garden culture which was linked to mercantile wealth was the creation of so-called "water-mouth gardens" (*shuikou yuan*), which were almost like small public parks or recreational areas created around the entrance of a water-course to a village (fig. 113). There can be little doubt that in many if not most cases these water-mouth gardens were developed through philanthropic contributions from wealthy local merchants. They marked the importance of the water source to the viability of the village settlement and had a *fengshui* purpose which can also be understood as an ecological value. In the present day, the residents of one such village, Hongcun, have revived their vernacular garden style as well as their entrepreneurial tradition, creating attractive small guest-houses for tourists (fig. 114).

An example of a man of Huizhou merchant origins who created a large garden and deployed it for cultural influence in a variety of ways during the late Ming was Wang Tingna, who was active around 1600. Unlike those Huizhou merchants who lived and worked in other parts of China before retiring back to their native soil, Wang Tingna himself seems to have remained resident in his home area throughout his life. He had evidently gained a good education based on his family's wealth, and was a man of multifarious talents, being a chess (*weiqi* or *go*) champion and a playwright as well as a publisher of luxury editions. He deployed his publishing business, which was based in his spacious garden, as a way of making contact with famous writers and intellectuals, whose work he published, often in woodblock reproduction of their own handwriting rather than in a regular print format. For example, a long description of his garden

Fig. 114 The "Hall of Virtue and Righteousness" (*Deyi tang*), a garden residence in Hongcun village.
(photo by Lei Gao)

Fig. 115 *Garden Scenes from the Hall Surrounded by Jade* (c. 1608; detail)
Qian Gong (artist); Huang Yingzu (engraver)
Woodblock-printed handscroll

On the extreme right of this section can be seen a small shrine to the Bodhisattva Guanyin above a lotus pond. A little to the left a path winds up a mound to a thatched pavilion known as the Plain Pavilion (*Su ting*). The hexagonal pavilion with the gourd-shaped entrance is named the Cavern for Observing Vacancy (*Guankong dong*). The first of these buildings represents Buddhism, the second Confucianism (with its values of plainness and simplicity), and the third Daoism; as a group they symbolize the syncretic belief popular in the late Ming of the "unity of the three doctrines."

was written by a well-known philosopher, Yuan Huang (1533–1606), and published in the elegant hand of the famous calligrapher Wang Zhideng (1535–1612) in a book entitled *Master Sitting-in-Reclusion's Compilation* (Master Sitting-in-Reclusion was one of Wang Tingna's studio names; it alludes through a classical quotation to his interest in chess).

Wang Tingna's garden was also illustrated in a remarkable woodblock-printed scroll (a very unusual type of artefact), which now survives only in facsimile (fig. 115). Smaller-scale illustrations of the garden also appear in another of Wang's luxury publications, *Master Sitting-in-Reclusion's Carefully Edited Manual of Chess Strategies* (fig. 116). These illustrations together with Yuan Huang's description make it clear that

Wang Tingna used his garden not only as a site for his publishing business and a place where he could get together with others to play chess, but also as an expression of his interest in the "unity of the three doctrines" of Confucianism, Daoism, and Buddhism (*sanjiao heyi*), a widespread philosophical approach in the late Ming. In this way also, he assimilated himself to the literati class.

Another member of a Huizhou merchant family was Zheng Yuanxun, whose garden was mentioned in Chapter Five; he was a minor landscape painter of the late Ming and a follower of the great art critic Dong Qichang, who gave Zheng's garden its name (fig. 117). Zheng's family had left Huizhou for good in a previous generation and settled in the

Fig. 116 Wang Tingna and friends in his garden, from Wang Geng's illustrations to *Master Sitting-in-Reclusion's Carefully Edited Manual of Chess Strategies*, edited by Wang Tingna

The chess player on the right may be Wang himself; the other player's distinctive cap suggests he is a Daoist, while the shaven-headed figure with the fly-whisk is a Buddhist monk. Alternatively, Wang may be the fascinated observer on the left of the group. As in fig. 115, we see the association of Daoism, Buddhism, and Confucianism. The figure on the left half of the illustration is certainly intended to be Wang: he is followed by a servant carrying a bundle of calligraphy or painting scrolls which he is going to display for his friends to appreciate, a characteristic activity in literati gardens, here being used by someone of merchant background to enhance his claim to literatus status.

prosperous commercial city of Yangzhou, at the junction of the Yangtze River and the Grand Canal, where many other Huizhou merchants based their businesses. Yangzhou owed much of its prosperity to the salt trade, dominated by Huizhou merchants, though it

Fig. 117 *Landscape* (1631)
Zheng Yuanxun
Hanging scroll, ink on paper
Height 125.2 cm, width 52 cm
Suzhou Museum

Zheng painted this landscape in the Garden of Shade, as his signature indicates. Having grown up in Yangzhou, amid the relatively flat landscape of northern Jiangsu, Zheng was excited by the idea of mountains, and his garden, like this painting, was an attempt to create a mountainous landscape for himself.

Fig. 118 *Spring Dawn in the Han Palace* (detail)
Qiu Ying
Ink and color on paper
Dimensions of the complete handscroll: height
30.6 cm, length 574.1 cm
Palace Museum, Taibei

In this long handscroll the Ming professional painter Qiu Ying, based in Suzhou, imagines the activities of inhabitants of the Han-dynasty imperial palace in Chang'an (present-day Xi'an); this detail shows part of the palace garden. Although it is intended as a historical scene, the layout, architecture, and clothing belong entirely to the Ming.

is not clear if the Zheng family was involved in this. At any rate they were a wealthy family: Zheng and his two brothers all owned substantial gardens in Yangzhou. The garden of one of his brothers survived the Ming-Qing transition, in which the rich city of Yangzhou suffered terribly, but Zheng Yuanxun's Garden of Shade (*Yingyuan*; also translated as Garden of Reflection or Reflections) seems to have been largely destroyed: only remnants survived into the Qing. Though he was from a merchant background, Zheng himself passed the highest level of the government examinations; we can see from Zheng's own description of his garden, which was designed by the celebrated garden designer Ji Cheng (see Chapter Eight), that it was intended to be an entirely suitable setting for the life of a literatus.

Women's Activities in Gardens

The story of Chinese gardens is often told as if it were a story of men only, and indeed of very few men other than emperors and literati. But a closer examination of the evidence shows that this was not the case at all. We have already seen that court ladies played an important part in the garden culture of the Tang dynasty (see Chapter Two), and that in the Song dynasty (see Chapter Three) elite women were able to visit other people's gardens in company with their husbands, while the gardens of their own families provided a setting for their everyday lives as well as a mirror of their emotional lives.

Examples of women's role in garden culture are more numerous in the late imperial period. Nevertheless, there is still much

less information than there is for the part played by elite men. In the case of women, we are forced to extrapolate from such evidence as we have and we may not always be correct in the conclusions we draw. We must always bear in mind that most of the evidence comes from descriptions or images created by male writers or artists, and may therefore represent a male fantasy about the lives of women in gardens rather than the

Fig. 119 Woodblock-printed illustration to a late-Ming edition of *The Peony Pavilion*

In a scene from the famous drama, Du Liniang searches in the garden for the young man with whom she fell in love in her dream. Lamenting her solitary state, she sees a beautiful prunus tree and vows that she will be buried beneath its branches. This illustration, quoting the line "Upstairs the blossoming branches shade me as I sleep alone," shows her asleep in her lonely bed.

actuality. This is particularly the case with fictional representations. A further difficulty is that the vast majority of the evidence we have—other than that reflecting or imagining the life of the imperial court (fig. 118)—comes from the economically advanced Jiangnan, where literacy among elite women was at a high level, so that even when we do have information from women themselves, we cannot know whether women in other parts of China had less to do with gardens or if they had just as much as the women of Jiangnan but left few or no written records.

From today's perspective, it is clear that gardens in the Ming dynasty were much less likely to be viewed as feminine spaces than in the Qing. During the Ming dynasty, the association between women and gardens was usually represented in fiction and drama as a source of danger: in the much-loved 16th-century drama *The Peony Pavilion or The Soul's Return (Mudan ting huanhun ji)*, after the heroine Du Liniang has ventured into the garden behind her father's official residence, she dreams of a romantic tryst with a handsome young man, resulting in her death from love-sickness (fig. 119; see also fig. 100 on page 84), while in the satirical novel *The Plum in the Golden Vase* all kinds of hanky-panky goes on in the anti-hero's garden, eventually contributing to his death and the collapse of his household. Although it may be partly a function of the type of evidence that has survived, it does seem that there was a transition in the very late Ming or early Qing from the garden being regarded as primarily a masculine space, where men held scholarly gatherings and carried out typically male activities often related to their social roles as scholar-officials, to a conception of the garden as a realm associated primarily with femininity. We will explore this further in Chapter Ten.

It is not easy to find information on the realities of women's role in the garden

culture of the Yuan or early Ming dynasties. A 14th-century lacquer tray (fig. 120) depicts a scene of two women and a number of children (boys) in a garden setting. The seated woman is the lady of the house and mother of at least some of the boys, while the standing woman holding a baby is probably either a nursemaid or a concubine (and in this case likely to be the birth mother of some of the children, though they would all be brought up to regard the principal wife as their mother). The scene, however, is not one of "real life" but a generic one of the auspicious type often seen in decorative art known as "the hundred children" (more precisely "the hundred sons," *bai zi*), representing the wish for a large family of male offspring. Often the theme is depicted through children only (fig. 121), so the presence of the two women here is slightly unusual. The lacquer piece probably dates from the late Yuan or perhaps the very early Ming; the style of the garden could belong to either period. It shows typical features such as the pavilion built over a lotus-pond surrounded by balustrades, Lake Tai rocks, a flowering tree of some sort on the right, and a willow on the left. A slightly incongruous element is the table set in front of the other rock, with what seem to be antique bronze and porcelain pieces displayed

Fig. 120   Carved red lacquer tray (14th century)
Diameter 55.6 cm, depth 6 cm
Metropolitan Museum of Art, New York

The auspicious design of children at play in a garden setting is beautifully carved, showing the high level of skill achieved by Yuan and early Ming lacquer craftsmen. The artist had a sense of humor as well: it is fun to see that the rock on the right is being used for a game of hide-and-seek, with one child crouched below it, while another's head can just be seen in the gap above him.

Fig. 121   Ming dynasty blue-and-white bowl with design of children at play in a garden
Height 15.2 cm, diameter of mouth 31.1 cm
Metropolitan Museum of Art, New York

The traditional auspicious design of "children at play," often called "the hundred children," depicts children enjoying various different games and activities in a garden environment, and expresses a wish for the good fortune of having many sons. The boys may be shown playing with toys, or they may be imitating adult activities such as a procession to celebrate the success of the top graduate in the government examinations, as in this image, with the "graduate" riding a hobby-horse and a playmate holding a lotus-leaf as a ceremonial parasol.

on it. This is an element that very often appears in paintings of "elegant gatherings" of gentlemen in a garden (fig. 122), but it seems rash to have it here: the little boy playing soldiers with the flag is bound to knock something over and break it. Perhaps the antiques are here to stand in for the presence of the lucky father of all these lively young fellows.

With the great expansion of female literacy and of publishing in the mid- to late Ming, more information on women and gardens becomes available to us. In the 15th and 16th centuries, especially, there seems to have been an association—at least in the minds of upper-class men—between women and the cultivation of fruit trees, presumably representing fertility, but perhaps also because women were more concerned with the production and use of fruit from the family's

Du Jin was a literatus who took up a career as an artist. His inscription on the painting makes clear that he regarded the appreciation of antiques as a way to gain insight into the past and thus refine one's character. The painting conveys this message through a clever variation on the theme of the "Four Accomplishments": playing the zither (*qin*), chess (*weiqi*), calligraphy, and (connoisseurship of) painting (compare fig. 126 on page 106). The woman on the upper right is unwrapping a (probably antique) zither, the servant on the lower left is bringing a chess-board and a rolled-up scroll of painting or calligraphy, while more scrolls lie on the table beside the two women. The women are probably to be understood as concubines of the seated host, whom he has trained to take care of his antique collection; thus the painting implies that the appreciation of fine things includes also the appreciation of beautiful women in a garden setting.

garden for culinary purposes. The famous Suzhou writer and painter Wen Zhengming (1470–1559) wrote a poem about a prunus tree planted by his step-grandmother, a Ms. Gu (1433–1463), in the grounds of her natal family's Fragrant Shadows Hall, in which he seems to identify the spirit of the lady with the flourishing of the "hundred years old" tree. Although the prunus (*Prunus mume*) was most often celebrated by literati for its fragrant blossom, its fruits were also used in preserves, so it had a productive as well as esthetic function in the garden. Similarly, an essay by Gui Youguang (1507–1571) paying tribute to three generations of women in his life (his grandmother, mother, and wife) notes that in the year she died, his wife had planted in the courtyard of their home a loquat tree which by the time of writing had "grown to a great height and spreads like a roof." The implication is that through the fruitful loquat tree (fig. 123), Mrs. Gui's spirit is still watching over the household.

Fig. 123 *Loquats*
Shen Zhou (1427–1509)
Album leaf, ink and color on paper
Height 27.8 cm, width 37.3 cm
Palace Museum, Beijing

The literatus artist Shen Zhou, like his close friend Wen Zhengming, was a leading figure in the "Suzhou school" of painting. Artists often produced albums depicting different flowers and fruits, showing their skill in catching and conveying the essence of these subjects. In Chinese medical lore, the loquat fruit has cooling properties, so it is particularly appreciated in the hot summers of the Yangtze delta region.

Fig. 124 *Lakeside Pavilion in a Bamboo Grove*
Li Rihua
Album leaf, ink and slight color on silk
Height 26.4 cm, width 29.5 cm
Harvard Art Museums

Li Rihua was a minor artist but a noted collector and connoisseur of art, whose diary gives us detailed information on the art market in late-Ming Jiangnan as well as on elite family life. In this painting, which he signed with his pen-name "Lazy among Bamboo" (Zhulan), he depicts an idyllic country residence among bamboo, the sort of place he would want his own villa to be. Bamboo, an indispensable part of every garden, appears frequently in works by literati because of its association with integrity (the Chinese word for a "joint" or "section" of bamboo, *jie*, is the same as the word for integrity) and the combination of moral strength and flexibility required of the scholar-official.

In the diary of the art collector and connoisseur Li Rihua (1565–1635), covering the years 1609–1616, we can catch glimpses of his wife's involvement in the cultivation of vegetables for the family table. In the 4th month of 1610, for example, the couple went together to their country villa outside the city of Jiaxing where they lived (Jiaxing is near Hangzhou). There they "arranged" or "took care of" the vegetable garden; they also "counted 620 stems of bamboo," presumably needing them for some practical purpose (fig. 124). Two months later they went back there to "pick lotuses and tidy up [stake and tie?] the runner beans." Li Rihua himself was very interested in flowers: he commented constantly on what was flowering in his own or other people's gardens. His wife seems to have shared this interest: in early 1616 Li and his wife, son, and grandson went to the country residence to pick red and white prunus blossom in the snow. On Mrs. Li's birthday in the 5th month of that year, pink and white lotuses were in bloom in their garden in Jiaxing, as were hollyhocks and pomegranates, and she and other female family members became quite tipsy while enjoying the sight.

As well as growing fruit and vegetables,

women may have been particularly involved in the cultivation of medicinal herbs. Women were certainly concerned with the preparation and provision of herbal remedies for female illnesses and troubles. The artist Wen Shu (1595–1634), a great-great-granddaughter of the celebrated Wen Zhengming, painted many images of day-lilies (fig. 125) for female friends and clients: day-lilies, in addition to being edible, were used in traditional medicine for pain relief in childbirth as well as for other female complaints such as mastitis, so women would often give each other such paintings to express good wishes for child-bearing. Wen Shu herself had one daughter but no son, so the day-lily may have had a particular significance for the artist. Wen Shu was closely associated with the well-known Hanshan Garden of her husband's family on the outskirts of Suzhou: an inscription by her husband on one of her paintings states "On fine days during spring and autumn in our mountain residence, every time there were fine and beautiful flowers decorating in between the rocks and mountains, my wife Wen Shu would paint them in ink and color."[20] Thus he emphasizes both the authenticity of her work and her status as a respectable wife secluded within her home, despite the fact that she sold her paintings to support the family finances.

One 17th-century gentrywoman about whose involvement in garden culture we know an unusually large amount was the poet Shang Jinglan (1605–c. 1676). Born into a noted scholar-official family in Shaoxing, Zhejiang, she became the wife of the distinguished late-Ming official Qi Biaojia (1603–1645), whose wealthy family owned several gardens in and around Shaoxing. Qi's diary, which covers the years 1631 to 1645, is a rich source of data on his family life and garden activities. Qi's own garden was the Yushan or Allegory Mountain Garden, situated about a mile outside the city walls (see fig. 94 on page 80). Qi

began to develop the garden while he was on leave in the mid-1630s, and Shang Jinglan was involved with the garden from an early stage, visiting the site with him while it was still being planned. The garden was large enough to contain a home farm, and in the account of his garden which Qi wrote on its completion, he describes accompanying his wife and children to take refreshments for the farm workers; he also claims that his wife spent time there during "silkworm season," gathering mulberry leaves to feed the silkworms. These eulogies of his wife's domestic virtue may not be entirely truthful, but they do suggest it was credible that a gentrywoman would have some involvement with agricultural or horticultural activity.

Shang Jinglan often spent time in the Yushan Garden with her husband, and since they were a very close couple, we can imagine that it was a relief for them to be there by

Fig. 126   Blue-and-white *guan* jar with illustrations of the "Four Accomplishments"
Xuande reign period (1426–1435), Ming dynasty
Diameter of mouth 22.1 cm, diameter of base 21.8 cm, height 34.4 cm
Shanghai Museum

The "Four Accomplishments" (see fig. 122 on page 103) are usually shown being practiced by men, but here they are undertaken by women. This was probably intended as a titillating subject for the male gaze, but at the same time such activity cannot have been unimaginable in real life. On this side of the jar, a lady seated in front of a screen between flowering trees and stylized garden rocks is admiring a landscape painting held up by a servant-girl. The other "accomplishments" are shown around the jar.

themselves, away from the pressures of the extended family home, not to mention the problems in her natal family, where her elderly father was becoming increasingly crotchety, and she was the only one of his children who seemed able to manage him. She also frequented Yushan and the other Qi family gardens together with female relatives, including her mother-in-law, aunts, and sisters-in-law, who often enjoyed family parties and celebrations which generally included watching theatrical performances (the Qi family had their own theater troupe, and Qi Biaojia was a noted expert on drama). In this way, the garden activities of these women mirrored the activities of male literati (fig. 126). In the same way as groups of male friends would visit gardens together, Shang Jinglan and her husband quite often visited other people's gardens together, particularly during 1635, though once their own garden was complete they seem to have made fewer visits to gardens elsewhere; it is possible that they were visiting the other gardens partly to gather ideas for the development of their own garden.

At the same time, groups of women from outside the family sometimes visited the Yushan Garden. On the Lantern Festival in 1637, "there were tourists all day, and groups of women. It was going like a fair: the garden has never been so lively." Qi even wrote a light-hearted poem describing how "Girls of eighteen with trailing silk sashes / Leave scented footprints at every step in the soil of the embankment" and "Stooping towards the ripples they view the reflections of their rosy faces." Sometimes, though, it was all too much: later in 1637, there were so many women visiting the garden one day that Qi Biaojia himself was forced to take refuge with the monk whose hermitage was next door.

These happy scenes in the garden came to an end after the Qing conquest, when in the summer of 1645 Qi decided that the only

way to avoid collaborating with the invaders without endangering his family was for him to commit suicide as a Ming loyalist; he did this by drowning himself in the Yushan Garden's large pond. Shang Jinglan was left a widow at the age of forty. Her surviving poems all seem to have been written after this cataclysmic event, and many of them use descriptions of the garden as a way of expressing her sadness and longing for her dead husband: "The old garden is a deserted, cheerless place; / Visiting it again, my longings are redoubled."

One woman who was decidedly not of gentry origins, but who was nevertheless received in the Yushan Garden as a guest of its owner, was the celebrated courtesan Liu Rushi (1618–1664). She visited the garden in the company of her then lover Wang Ranming (1577–1655), who was a wealthy Huizhou merchant, living in Hangzhou and socializing with local literati. Both Liu and Wang wrote poems on the garden; Liu's refers to a pavilion named the Flute Pavilion, whose musical association may have seemed suitable for a performing artist, as courtesans usually were. However, only Wang's poem appears in the collection which Qi published of poems on the garden written by his friends and acquaintances; Liu's poem appears in her own poetry collection, *Grass on the Lake* or *Lakeside Jottings* (*Hushang cao*).

The connection of courtesans with garden culture has some interesting aspects. Like those of gentrywomen, the garden activities of high-class courtesans in the late Ming to early Qing show similarities to those of elite men. They might hold or attend garden parties with their friends: Ma Shouzhen (1548–1604), one of the leading courtesans of Nanjing, borrowed or hired a garden in Suzhou for a party to celebrate the seventieth birthday of her friend and former lover, the calligrapher Wang Zhideng, a native of Suzhou. She herself is said to have had a garden residence in Nanjing with flowers and a few well-chosen rocks set beside water (fig. 127).

Another courtesan in late-Ming Nanjing noted for the elegance of her garden was Li Xiangzhen, known as Tenth Lady Li (Li Shiniang). According to a description written towards the end of the 17th century by someone who had known her in her heyday, her garden contained a single old prunus tree, two wutong trees, and about ten stems of giant bamboo: in other words, its restrained design was the last word in fashionable garden style. She was noted for washing the wutong trees every day, in emulation of the famous Yuan-dynasty painter Ni Zan (see Chapter Four), who had an obsession for cleanliness (fig. 128). Thus she, too, was laying claim to elite status.

Courtesans like Ma Shouzhen and Tenth Lady Li evidently used their garden residences as showcases for their own charm, elegance, and sophistication. But courtesans could also use their gardens not just as social and cultural capital but as actual financial capital, even though under imperial law women were not supposed to own property. Shen Defu, in his *Private Gleanings of the Wanli Era*, tells the sad story of a courtesan who had made a substantial investment in a garden property. Shen and another man, Fan, were taken by a mutual friend to meet her in her grand house and garden somewhere outside Beijing, in the hope (on her part) of making a match. Shen was not interested in a relationship, so he made his excuses and left. He was surprised when, some years later, the friend who had introduced them accused him of ruining the woman's life. The friend explained that, failing to attract Shen, she had taken up with Fan, who gambled away all her savings, so she had to sell all her property including her mansion and garden. She was driven to suicide when the untrustworthy Fan eventually left her, and Fan himself later came to a well-deserved bad end.

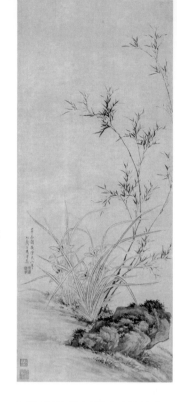

Fig. 127 *Ink Orchids after Guan Daosheng* (1572)
Ma Shouzhen
Hanging scroll
Height 95.5 cm, width 38 cm
Shanghai Museum

Orchids (cymbidium), with their elegance and delicate fragrance, were a favored subject for paintings by courtesans, who were often trained artists as well as musical performers; Ma Shouzhen is noted for her ink renderings of the plant. In her inscription on this literati-style composition of orchids, bamboo, and rock, Ma says it is a "study" or "copy" of the style of "Madame Guan," the Yuan-dynasty artist Guan Daosheng, famous for her paintings of bamboo (see fig. 70 on page 61).

Fig. 128 *Ni Zan Washing a Wutong Tree*
Cui Zizhong (1574–1644)
Hanging scroll, ink and color on silk
Height 160 cm, width 53 cm
Palace Museum, Taibei

Ni Zan, accompanied by a female attendant and her maid, stands beside a massive garden rock, supervising the scrubbing of a wutong tree by two servants.

CHAPTER EIGHT
GARDEN DESIGN AND CREATION

Fine gardens do not come into existence without a great deal of planning and hard work. Planning of a garden may be done by the owner, but even so, it takes skill to translate the plan into the reality of an effective layout on the ground. Then there is the skill required to construct the necessary buildings, water-courses, pools, and rockwork, as well as to plant the right types of vegetation and perhaps to transplant or prune existing trees, not to mention taking care of the plants by watering, weeding, removing pests, and so on. Who did all this work in Chinese gardens?

We have no information at all on garden craftsmen in the Tang or Song dynasties. We saw in Chapter Four that in the Yuan period, the rockery in the monastery garden which preceded the present Lion Grove garden in Suzhou may have been planned or even designed by a group of literati, who were brought together by the monk in charge of the site. Nevertheless, they must have needed a rockery expert and construction workers to turn it into a reality, yet there is no mention of these men's contribution.

Even in the early Ming, we hear nothing about garden craftsmen, though it is difficult if not impossible to imagine the literati garden owners who wrote so extensively about their gardens actually rolling up their sleeves, kilting up their robes, and undertaking the physical labor. It is only from the 16th century that the names of garden craftsmen start

to appear in the textual record. This is no coincidence, since we have seen that this was just the time when the popularization of new philosophical ideas was changing attitudes towards the identity of the individual, and when economic development was driving social change and enhancing social mobility. It is not only garden craftsmen whose names start to become known: for example, the potters who made the distinctive "purple clay" teapots of Yixing on the other side of Lake Tai from Suzhou began signing their work at this time (figs. 129 and 130), and

Figs. 129 and 130 Yixing ware teapot
Shi Dabin (fl. 1620–1640)
Height 9.5 cm
Metropolitan Museum of Art, New York

The shape of the teapot suggests the five-petalled prunus flower, but also resembles a melon. It is signed on the base by the potter, Shi Dabin, one of the first potters to sign his work, as "Dabin of the Jade Radiance Belvedere," this presumably being the name of his studio or workshop (see the detail on the right).

literati authors started to describe items attributed to specific craftsmen as particularly collectible. It is also no coincidence, given the dominance of culture in the Ming by inhabitants of the Jiangnan region, that up till the very early Qing, the only garden craftsmen we know of were based in Jiangnan. Even so, the fact remains that our knowledge is almost entirely about garden craftsmen who were categorized as rockery experts, and we know almost nothing of individual plantsmen, although such a profession certainly existed.

Fig. 131 Rockery in the Yu Garden, Shanghai, designed by Zhang Nanyang for Pan Yunduan in the 1560s. The rockery is formed not of Lake Tai rocks, frequently used for smaller-scale rockwork or individually displayed rocks, but of "yellow rocks" (*huangshi*) which are much bulkier and sturdier, making possible larger and more stable constructions.

Rockwork Craftsmen

The first garden craftsman whose full name we know was Zhang Nanyang, who worked in the mid- to late 16th century; he was also known as "the Mountain Man who Reclines upon Rocks (*Woshi shanren*)." Surprisingly, one of his rockwork creations survives to this day. This is the large rockery "mountain" in the Yu Garden, or Pleasurable Garden, in Shanghai, which Zhang created for its first owner, Pan Yunduan (fig. 131). Pan Yunduan (1506–?) was a senior official whose home was in Shanghai; he planned the garden as a retreat for his father's old age, but his father died before it was completed, so he occupied it himself. We know of at least two other gardens designed by Zhang Nanyang, one in Shanghai named the Daily Visit Garden (*Rishe yuan*) for Chen Suoyun, who wrote a short biography of Zhang, and one in Taicang near Suzhou, the Yanzhou or Yanshan Garden of Wang Shizhen (see Chapter Five and fig. 95 on page 81). According to the biography by Chen Suoyun, Zhang was working on Pan's and Wang's gardens at the same time, shuttling back and forth between Shanghai and Taicang and balancing the competing demands of his two influential clients. We know from Wang

Shizhen's account of his Yanzhou Garden that in addition to Zhang's work, other parts of the garden were designed by a Mr. Wu and a Mr. Cao: Wang says that their work and Zhang's was all equally good. Nothing more is known of Mr. Wu, but it is possible that Mr. Cao was Cao Liang, a Shanghai native whom Chen Suoyun employed to complete the Daily Visit Garden after the death of Zhang Nanyang; Chen also says that there was nothing to choose between Cao Liang's work and Zhang's.

We are told that Zhang Nanyang had begun by studying painting, his father having become known as a skilled artisan painter, but that he then turned his painting technique to the design of rockwork. Chen Suoyun's biography gives a vivid sense of the power of Zhang's creativity and of his personality:

The mountains formed themselves into mighty peaks, winding and extending, lofty and up-thrusting, steep and jagged, rearing intermittently, rising and falling, twisting and turning, mighty and forceful. Overall they appeared like a huge mass extended over a vast distance, although they were on a small scale. … From high to low, from great to small, he created their form

in accordance with the lie of the land; as though without any preliminary cogitation, the mountains thrust upwards in a myriad wondrous shapes. Those who saw them were astounded and stunned, and declared that they could not come from the world of men. The Mountain Man, too, when things came out exactly right, would often shout aloud in satisfaction and exclaim that the gods had helped him.[21]

Zhang gained so much prestige that wealthy garden owners clamored for his services. In order to attract him they would send their carriages to convey him to their homes rather than having him make his own way there, as would normally be expected of an artisan. His forthright personality enabled him to avoid accepting commissions from those with whom he disagreed or who he feared would

Fig. 132   Ding ware lidded bowl with lotus petal design

Five Dynasties period (907–960)
Height 7.8 cm, diameter at widest point 9.2 cm
Shanghai Museum

This bowl, with its pattern of lotus petals incised into the clay under the white glaze and the lid handle in the form of a flower stem, represents the type of ceramic which Zhou Shichen became known for reproducing.

Fig. 133   The Garden for Lingering, Suzhou, Jiangsu Province

This site was the garden of the Xu family just outside the walls of Suzhou city. After two centuries in the ownership of the Xu family, it passed in the late 18th century into the ownership of a family named Liu and was popularly known as the Liu Garden. About a hundred years later, after being damaged in the Taiping Rebellion (1850–1864), it became the property of the Sheng family, who reconstructed it and renamed it Garden for Lingering (*Liu yuan* in Chinese, but with a different Liu character from the Liu of the previous owners). It has been suggested that rockwork in the north-western corner of the Garden for Lingering (to the far left of this image) is a remnant of Zhou Shichen or Zhou Tingce's work.

get him into any kind of difficulty. Chen Suoyun tells us that Zhang enjoyed a healthy life to the age of 100.

Around the same time, in Suzhou, lived a craftsman named Zhou Shichen (also known as Zhou Bingzhong and Zhou Danquan). His exact dates are unknown (he lived from the early 16th to early 17th century), but he is recorded in various sources as a maker of ceramic seals in the style of antique Ding ware (a type of white-glazed ceramic), a skilled maker of reproduction antique porcelain with which he often fooled unwary collectors (fig. 132), and a designer of *penjing*. Yuan Hongdao (1568–1610), a famous writer who served as an official in Suzhou, attributes to Zhou a large rockery screen "like a horizontal landscape scroll" in the Xu family's garden in the north-eastern suburbs of Suzhou. This garden was on the site where the Garden for Lingering (*Liu yuan*) now stands (fig. 133), with the rockery in its north-west corner. A member of the Xu family, Xu Shupi (1596–1683), remembered Zhou Shichen as a somewhat eccentric old man when he (Xu) was young, but he does not say anything to connect him with garden design. On the other hand, he mentions Zhou's son Tingce as a rockery craftsman much admired in Suzhou, so it is likely that Yuan Hongdao (who did not stay long in Suzhou, disliked the city, and was not much interested in gardens) was wrong about the Xu rockery and it was actually created by Zhou Tingce.

Towards the end of the Ming dynasty, there was another craftsman with a range of skills who also designed at least one garden in the Jiangnan area. This was Zhu Zhizheng, also known as "Third Pine-tree" Zhu (Zhu Sansong, fl. c. 1573–1619), who is best known as a bamboo carver (fig. 134). His grandfather Zhu He (the first "Pine-tree") appears to have established the family bamboo carving business in Jiading (now part of Shanghai Municipality), which was a center of this craft. Zhu He is said to have been a calligrapher, painter, and seal cutter also. Zhu He's son Zhu Ying (1520–1587), the "Younger Pine-tree" (Zhu Xiaosong) specialized in the carving of Buddhas

Fig. 134   Incense holder with scholars in a landscape

Zhu Sansong
Bamboo, height 17.8 cm
Metropolitan Museum of Art, New York

This bamboo piece is signed by Zhu Sansong. One can imagine that Zhu's skill in depicting landscape within the constraints of this medium would encourage his patrons to believe in his landscape design skills and thus commission him to design a garden.

Fig. 135   The Guyi Garden or Ancient Garden of Elegance in Nanxiang of Jiading, Shanghai

Zhu Sansong's original concept for the garden of Min Shiji was probably lost in a major reconstruction by later owners in the mid-18th century. At the end of the 18th century, it became a semi-public garden attached to the local City God's Temple. After having suffered considerable damage, it was restored in the 1980s under the supervision of Professor Chen Congzhou, one of the 20th century's greatest experts on Chinese gardens; it was further extended in the 2000s.

and Daoist immortals in bamboo and wood. Zhu Ying's son Sansong, as well as carrying on the family trade of bamboo carving, became an artist specializing in paintings of rocks and bamboo, and it was perhaps for this reason that in the mid-16th century an official named Min Shiji commissioned him to design the Garden of Elegance (*Yi yuan*) in Nanxiang, which is quite near the Zhus' hometown Jiading. The garden, now known as the Ancient Garden of Elegance (*Gu Yiyuan*), was sensitively reconstructed in the 1980s (fig. 135).

Fig. 136 *Twisting Bridge and Solitary Pavilion (1340)*
Wu Zhen
Album leaf, ink on paper
Height 27.7 cm, width 58.6 cm
Palace Museum, Taibei

Zhang Lian's style as a landscape designer was compared to the work of the Yuan master Wu Zhen. This landscape painting by Wu Zhen suggests the sort of impression that might be made on visitors to gardens designed by Zhang.

Garden Designers—Zhang Lian and Ji Cheng

In the early 17th century, around the end of Zhu Sansong's active career, a family of garden creators emerged in the city of Jiaxing, in northern Zhejiang, who dominated their industry for several generations. They can be regarded as true garden designers or landscape architects, rather than simple rockery craftsmen. They were the Zhang family, who became known as the "Mountain Zhangs" (*Shanzi Zhang*). The first member of the family to take up garden design as a profession was Zhang Lian (1587–after 1650), also known by his formal name as Zhang Nanyuan. He should not be confused with Zhang Nanyang, who was no relation, but, like his predecessor, Zhang Lian was another powerful personality. It used to be thought that Zhang Lian was from an artisan background, but evidence has recently come to light showing that he was from a family of literati; however, against his father's wishes, he abandoned the quest for an official career (which he may have felt was going nowhere)

and turned to his real passion, the creation of gardens. He was on friendly terms with some of the leading literati of Jiangnan, including the poet Wu Weiye (1609–1671/2), who wrote his biography. He is known to have designed gardens for many prominent literati including the writer and painter Wang Shimin (1592–1680) and the leading literary man of the time, Qian Qianyi (1582–1664). The art critic Dong Qichang compared his style to that of the great Yuan-dynasty landscape painters Huang Gongwang (1269–1354) and Wu Zhen (1280–1354) (fig. 136).

We are lucky to have a set of paintings of the garden designed by Zhang Lian for Wang Shimin. This was a garden known as Pleasure in the Suburbs (*Lejiao yuan*), situated just outside the city walls of Taicang, where Wang lived. In the account of the garden which Wang wrote for his sons after the Qing conquest, he humorously claimed that the amount of time and money which he spent on developing the garden was all Zhang Lian's fault. In 1625, when

Fig. 137 *Cool Heart Hall* Leaf from the album *Twelve Views of a Suburban Garden* (1625)

Shen Shichong
Palace Museum, Taibei

The name of the Cool Heart Hall reflects the owner Wang Shimin's Buddhist beliefs. The design of this part of the Pleasure in the Suburbs garden reflects the style that we know from other sources (principally Wu Weiye's biography of Zhang Lian) was typical of Zhang Lian: the winding rocky banks of the stream, crossed by a simple rustic bridge, are particularly characteristic.

Fig. 138 *Moonlit Embankment and Misty Willows* (1642)

Liu Rushi (1618–1664)
Handscroll, ink and color on paper
Palace Museum, Beijing

This painting of Caressing the Waters Mountain Villa, like fig. 137, shows what we understand to be Zhang Lian's typically understated, naturalistic style of garden design, with an open layout, where rockwork structures were intended to suggest the presence of mountains in the wider environment, rather than reproducing complete mountains on a small scale. A comment on the painting by Qian Qianyi, saying that Liu Rushi "depicted" or "drew" (*tu*) rather than "painted" (*hua*) the garden, implies that this was a fairly true-to-life representation.

the garden was more or less complete, he commissioned the artist Shen Shichong to depict it in a set of album leaves (fig. 137; see also fig. 97 on page 82). We also have an image of Qian Qianyi's Caressing the Waters Mountain Villa (*Fushui shanzhuang*) in nearby Changshu (fig. 138), painted in 1642 by Qian's concubine, the celebrated former courtesan Liu Rushi, who was better known as a poet than as an artist (see Chapter Seven).

Zhang Lian's sons and possibly a nephew followed him into the landscape gardening profession. One of his sons, Zhang Yifan, was involved in the design of the Yushan Garden in Shaoxing (see fig. 94 on page 80). Zhang Ran, Lian's fourth and youngest son, became the best known of this generation of the Mountain Zhangs; as we will see in Chapter 11, he had a stellar career in the early Qing

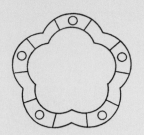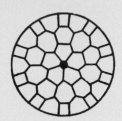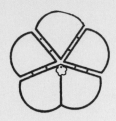

dynasty working on the imperial gardens in Beijing.

We know about Zhang Lian and the Zhang family from others who wrote about them, but there is another garden designer, a contemporary and probable rival of Zhang Lian, whom we know primarily from his own writing. This was Ji Cheng (1582–after 1635), who wrote the first theoretical treatise on garden design in China, *The Craft of Gardens* (*Yuanye*). This book, which was probably intended to advertise Ji Cheng's services rather than to give away his trade secrets, is quite vague on the actual process of garden design, but full of poetic descriptions of the artistic effects to be achieved by the skilled designer. It also contains a large number of diagrams of decorative lattice-work, balustrades, door and window shapes, and

Fig. 139   Diagrams from Ji Cheng's *Craft of Gardens* (c. 1635)

The leftmost figure shows the plan of a prunus-blossom shaped pavilion, with the pillars marked in the curved sections, while the diagram on the far right of the figure shows Ji's design for opening prunus-blossom-shaped window shutters. Zheng Yuanxun's record of his Garden of Shade, which was designed by Ji Cheng, mentions a prunus-blossom shaped pavilion, so these diagrams may well be based on the designs he created for Zheng.

other features, which we can be confident represented the latest styles at the time of publication in the 1630s (fig. 139). The use of windows and doorways of a variety of shapes and forms appears to have started only at this time, along with the changes in garden style described in Chapter Five; there is no evidence from earlier times even of the round "moon-door" or "moon-gate," which is now thought of as an essential element of Chinese gardens (fig. 140). One small pond in Mi Wanzhong's Ladle Garden (see Chapter Five) is described as being in the shape of a crescent moon, with the buildings surrounding it also having windows of a crescent-moon shape. As we will see in Chapter 11, the

Fig. 140   Moon-gate in the Garden of Cultivation (*Yipu*), Suzhou, Jiangsu Province

The present garden is on the site of a late-Ming garden belonging to a scion of the distinguished Wen family of Suzhou, Wen Zhenheng (1585–1645). He was the author of *A Treatise on Superfluous Things* (*Zhangwu zhi*), a book on elegant living in which he lays down the law about what is appropriate (or not) in a gentleman's garden. The garden is believed to retain many of its original late-Ming features, though whether this moon-gate is one of them is uncertain. Moon-gates were a design feature introduced only in the very late Ming; they became even more popular during the Qing.

17ᵗʰ-century author and garden designer Li Yu (1611–1680) claimed to have invented the idea of a fan-shaped window, another feature which now seems very typical of Chinese gardens. It seems likely that this fashion for elaborate forms of window and door, often paired with particular forms of carved decoration and even shapes of pavilion (such as a pavilion with a floor-plan in the shape of a five-petalled plum blossom, with five-lobed windows and sprays of plum blossom carved in the woodwork), was introduced to balance the increased simplicity of the garden design as a whole. These new demands from garden designers and owners must have required builders and woodworkers to develop new construction and carving techniques.

Ji Cheng, not unlike Zhang Lian, was probably an educated man who was obliged by economic necessity to earn his living in a profession usually undertaken by artisans, hence his ability to write about his profession. The book was supplied with prefaces by two of his clients, Ruan Dacheng (1587–1646), a poet, dramatist, and former official who had been dismissed in the factional conflicts of the 1620s, and Zheng Yuanxun (see Chapters Five and Seven), an educated man who had not achieved office, for whom Ji Cheng designed the Garden of Shade in Yangzhou in the early 1630s. Ruan Dacheng also undertook the publication of Ji's book through his in-house publishing operation at his home in Anqing (in present-day Anhui Province). Ji Cheng designed a garden for Ruan Dacheng's father in Nanjing, where the family moved in 1635 as social unrest spread through the rural areas around Anqing. Ruan also wrote a number of poems for Ji Cheng, claiming him as a friend and complimenting his design skills, while Zheng praised his abilities as a designer in his description of the Garden of Shade. We also know of some other gardens which Ji Cheng designed, but no further information about them has been preserved.

Water and Plants

Some of the skills which garden craftsmen used were related to other areas of traditional technology, such as water management. We have already seen how, in quite early times, the beautiful landscape of the West Lake outside Hangzhou developed partly a result of the management of the lake as a water-supply, irrigation, and flood control resource. In Ji Cheng's *Craft of Gardens*, he gives advice on how rainwater runoff from a roof can be used to produce the effect of a waterfall. Temporary waterfalls could also be created with the installation of a holding tank at the top of a rockery (fig. 141). This would require a team of workers to fill the tank and keep refilling it as long as the garden's owner required the waterfall to flow.

Fig. 141   Stone holding tank for water, installed on a rockery in the garden of the Tianyige Library in Ningbo, Zhejiang Province
The Tianyige (Heavenly Unity Belvedere) was established as a private library in the 16ᵗʰ century, with an extensive garden. This water-tank has a hole (visible on the left) which could be plugged to retain water, or unplugged to create a temporary waterfall over the rockery. (photo by author)

Another well-developed field of knowledge in late imperial China was botany. Chinese gardeners had developed grafting and other horticultural techniques as early as the Tang dynasty; the late-Ming literatus and bon viveur Wen Zhenheng (1585–1645), owner of the Garden of Cultivation (*Yipu*) in Suzhou (see fig. 140 on page 115), thought that garden owners should familiarize themselves with the ancient methods of cultivating orchids and chrysanthemums, which "should be drawn upon for the instruction of gardeners."[22] Practitioners of traditional Chinese medicine paid particularly close attention to the properties of plants used in herbal treatments. It is not surprising, therefore, that commercial horticulture was highly developed in China by the late imperial period. We know that Suzhou was a particular center of the horticultural trade, supplying not only plants and rocks but even deer and cranes to enhance the magical atmosphere of a garden.

Qi Biaojia (see fig. 94 on page 80 and Chapter Seven) records in his diary commissioning tree specialists to provide and plant well-grown trees, as well as buying smaller plants and saplings from nursery gardens. On one occasion in the autumn of 1636, he went to buy some plants from an old woman in the neighborhood of his garden, obtaining several varieties, including a prunus tree (*Prunus mume*) which he had particularly been looking for. He does not record any more about the woman; presumably she was a widow—otherwise Qi would have dealt with her husband—running a nursery garden to support herself. Qi also received presents of various plants from friends and relatives, to whom he reciprocated with gifts of plants from his own garden.

In Shaoxing, where Qi lived, there was a plantsman named Jin Rusheng who lived in a small house with a garden called "Also a Garden" (*Yeshi yuan*), where Qi tells us "he

Fig. 142   Octagonal porcelain bowl (early to mid-17th century)

Formerly Butler Family Collection (photograph courtesy of the late Sir Michael Butler)

Although many Chinese porcelain pieces depict plants, flowers, and garden scenes, it is rather unusual to see a depiction of actual work being done in a garden, as here, where a gardener's assistant is watering a potted plant. All too often the hard work done by those who got their hands dirty in the garden is ignored in Chinese garden history.

raises several hundred flower specimens, most of them from unusual places and of the rarest variety, such that even experienced gardeners cannot identify them."[23] Qi's friend Zhang Dai also admired Jin's horticultural skill, describing how a seemingly endless series of blooms succeeded each other in his garden with the passing of the seasons and how Jin, though in poor health, expended great efforts to eradicate any pests that could damage the plants. From a letter written by Zhang to Jin to request various plants, preserved in a collection of Zhang's writing, it seems that Jin was a literatus whom the great and the good of Shaoxing such as Zhang and Qi regarded as an equal, even though he was evidently impoverished and made a living through his lowly occupation as a plantsman.

Garden workers were also needed to carry out routine unskilled work, keeping the paths swept and tidy and watering the plants (fig. 142). Qi Biaojia's diary entries often record orders to the servants to sweep the paths before visits to his garden by his family and friends. Such tasks may not have required great skill, but they were still an essential contribution to the maintenance of gardens.

PART III
GARDENS OF THE LATE IMPERIAL PERIOD—QING DYNASTY

In some respects the Manchu Qing dynasty resembled the Mongol Yuan dynasty which preceded the Ming, as a "conquest dynasty" in which non-Han invaders ruled China. However, the Qing rulers were much more dependent on the employment of Han-Chinese officials and military men, many of whom were already settled in Manchuria and had accompanied the Qing army on its advance into China.

Although anti-Manchu feeling among the Han-Chinese population was quite intense at the very beginning and end of the dynasty, for most of the time—and particularly during the highly prosperous 18th century—the two ethnic groups co-existed successfully. The culture of the Han-Chinese elite during the early decades of the dynasty showed little variation from that of the late Ming, but once the "conquest generation" had died out, the culture started to move in new directions, which were reflected in garden culture also. At the same time, many of the increasingly sinicized Manchu elite developed an enthusiastic appreciation of Chinese gardens.

By the mid-19th century, the incursions of Western and Japanese imperialism, combined with internal problems, put great pressure on Chinese government and society. Ideas about modernization derived from Japan and the West introduced changes to Chinese culture and ways of life. Foreign elements started to appear even in otherwise traditional Chinese gardens, while in the great "semi-colonial" industrial cities such as Shanghai new patterns of urban living created a demand for new styles of both public and private gardens.

Fig. 143   Please refer to fig. 149 on page 125.

CHAPTER NINE
THE EVOLUTION OF IMPERIAL GARDENS

After the conquest of Beijing in 1644, the new Qing rulers were able to take over the imperial palaces and parks which had been constructed under the Ming in the early 15th century, and to maintain approximately the same structure as in the Ming: although some buildings had become dilapidated, Beijing had not suffered extensive damage during the conquest.

Gardens of the Imperial Palace

The Qing emperors generally retained the Ming layout of the Imperial Flower Garden (*Yuhuayuan*) in the northern part of the Forbidden City (the residential part of the palace), and similarly kept the Western Park very much as it was under the Ming;

Fig. 144 *Lotus Country in Clear summer, in the Style of Zhao Lingrang* (1622)

Lan Ying (c. 1585–1664)
Album leaf, ink and color on silk
Height 32.4 cm, width 55.7 cm
Palace Museum, Taibei

Zhao Lingrang (fl. 1080–1100) was a painter of the very late Northern Song and a member of the Song imperial family. Part of the Ming imperial Western Park in its decline was thought to resemble a scene of Jiangnan by Zhao; this late-Ming painting suggests how an observer in the late Ming to early Qing might have envisaged such a scene.

this park covered the area of the present-day Beihai Park (Northern Sea) and Zhongnanhai (Central and Southern Seas) government complex, to the north and west of the palace. In a description of the Western Park published in 1684, Gao Shiqi (1644–1703) noted that the former Ming imperial parks outside the Forbidden City had been opened up to general use by the Qing emperors (though this was later reversed); Gao, whose home was in Zhejiang, was employed as supervisor of the Household Administration of the Heir Apparent, and from 1677 was able to live in the Western Park, so he became very familiar with it. Regarding the north-eastern bank of the Northern Sea, where the boat-houses for the Ming imperial boats had stood, he comments: "Now they are in ruins. In the cold dews of autumn, the wild mallards and withered lotus-leaves appear indistinctly among the rushy islets and reedy shores, not unlike a Jiangnan landscape painting by [the Song painter] Zhao Lingrang" (fig. 144). It is clear that the imperial gardens had fallen into considerable disrepair during the dynastic transition.

As a result, a substantial building programme was undertaken, replacing many of the dilapidated Ming buildings with new structures, including a Lama-Buddhist temple on Qionghua Island with its famous white stupa which can still be seen (fig. 145). Qing support for Lama Buddhism marked the importance to the dynasty of their Manchu culture and their links with Tibet and inner Asia. The Manchus originally followed

Fig. 145   The white stupa on Qionghua Island in Beihai Park was built in the very early Qing dynasty as part of a Tibetan-style Lama-Buddhist temple

shamanistic beliefs but had also adopted Tibetan Buddhism. The Kangxi Emperor (1654–1722, r. 1661–1722) took a great liking to the area of the Southern Sea, so he had it walled off and used it essentially as his office, carrying out government business there rather than within the palace itself. The Jiangnan rockery expert Zhang Ran (see Chapters Eight and Eleven) was brought in to lay out the gardens and rockwork in this area.

Another type of "garden" to adorn the imperial palace in the Qing dynasty was the illusory gardens created through the European technique of *trompe-l'oeil* painting, introduced to the court by the Jesuit missionaries, especially Giuseppe Castiglione (Chinese name Lang Shining, 1688–1766), who were employed as court artists and who were also involved in the creation of the "European Palaces" in the Garden of Perfect Brightness (*Yuanming yuan*, see page 125). Some impressive examples of such painting can be seen, now carefully and authentically restored, in the part of the Forbidden City known as the Palace of Tranquil Longevity (*Ningshou gong*), created for the retirement of the Qianlong Emperor after his abdication in 1796 (he abdicated out of respect for his grandfather the Kangxi Emperor to avoid exceeding Kangxi's sixty-year reign). The *trompe-l'oeil* murals here were probably painted by Castiglione's student Wang Youxue. They were painted on panels of silk which were then affixed to the walls and ceiling. In the "Studio of Exhaustion from Diligent Service" (*Juanqin zhai*), the ceiling decoration takes the form of a bamboo trellis covered with grape-vines, while the walls suggest that the chamber, which contains a small stage building where plays could be performed for the amusement of the emperor, opens out into a garden which can be seen beyond an illusory bamboo fence (fig. 146). The room thus gives the impression of being a vine arbor set in a garden, rather than within four walls. There is in fact a real garden outside, surrounded by the palace buildings.

The Summer Palace (*Yihe Yuan*)

The area around the Ming-dynasty Gold Hill Traveling Palace, to the north-west of Beijing, also remained a place of recreation for the use of the Qing emperors, but it was not until the mid-Kangxi period, once the remaining resistance to Qing rule had been suppressed in the 1680s, that resources and time were available to start developing the area further. In 1750, the Qianlong Emperor built a substantial Buddhist monastery on a pre-existing monastic site in honor of the sixtieth birthday of his mother; as sixty years represent a "cycle" of time, the sixtieth birthday is of great significance in Chinese culture. The lake was considerably enlarged and the spoil used to extend the hill, now renamed Longevity Hill (*Wanshou shan*). Construction work on the park itself, now named the Garden of Clear Ripples (*Qingyi yuan*), was not completed until 1761 (see fig. 2 on pages 2 and 3). As part of this process, an area of the park (now known as *Xiequ yuan* or Garden of Harmony) was designed to resemble the Jichang Garden in Wuxi (see fig. 15 on page 14). The Qianlong Emperor had been so delighted by what he saw of the gardens of Jiangsu and Zhejiang that he also gave orders for parts of these gardens

Fig. 146   The "Studio of Exhaustion from Diligent Service" in the Palace of Tranquil Longevity, Forbidden City, Beijing

A successful collaboration between the Palace Museum and the World Monuments Fund from 2002 to 2008 led to the complete restoration of this "studio" with its illusory garden, originally constructed in the 1770s in preparation for the Qianlong Emperor's retirement; the collaboration was extended to restoration of other parts of the Palace of Tranquil Longevity, including its real garden.

Fig. 147 This image, printed in Suzhou around 1740, shows lively activity on the streets and canals of Suzhou. It was this bustling commercial scene, the epitome of the flourishing Jiangnan economy, which the Qianlong Emperor wished to reproduce in the Garden of Clear Ripples and elsewhere. (The Bodleian Libraries, University of Oxford)

to be reproduced or imitated elsewhere in the imperial gardens of Beijing and the summer retreat at Chengde. Thus the gardens of southeast China—whether owned by literati or by upwardly mobile merchants—came to have a significant influence on the style of Qing imperial gardens. Prior to this, imperial gardens seem to have been quite distinct in style from Jiangnan gardens. Now, however, in addition to the influence of literati garden style on imperial gardens, the splendors of imperial gardens were echoed in private or temple gardens as they were up-graded to receive and accommodate the emperor on his travels.

Other echoes of Jiangnan also appeared in the Garden of Clear Ripples: the western embankment of the lake was intended to resemble the Su Embankment on Hangzhou's West Lake, while the north-western part of the park included a "Suzhou Street" where the emperor and his household would play at making purchases in "shops" staffed by palace eunuchs (fig. 147). Suzhou was known as one of the most commercially prosperous cities in the empire, and its economic prosperity could be seen as an outcome of the emperor's wise rule, so it is not surprising that the Qianlong Emperor—always attentive to his image— wanted to incorporate a reminder of it in this garden.

The Garden of Clear Ripples gained its present name of *Yihe yuan* (Garden for Maintaining Harmony) when it was reconstructed, after its destruction in the Second Opium War, to celebrate the sixtieth birthday of the Empress Dowager Cixi (1835– 1908) in 1895, allegedly with the use of funds allocated to the improvement of the Chinese navy. It is generally known in English as the Summer Palace, since in the later part of the dynasty the imperial household moved there for the duration of the hot Beijing summers.

The Garden of Expansive Springtime (*Changchun Yuan*)

"Suzhou Streets" like those of the Summer Palace were also constructed for imperial amusement in two other imperial parks in this area, the Garden of Expansive Springtime and the Garden of Perfect Brightness. The Garden of Expansive Springtime was the first of the major Qing imperial gardens to be constructed in this area to the north of the county town of Haidian, beginning in the mid-1680s (fig. 148). It was laid out on the site occupied by the Marquis of Wuqing's garden in the late Ming (see Chapter Six), making use of what remained of the garden's features in line with the Kangxi Emperor's customary frugality. The design was inspired by the gardens which the emperor had seen on his first tour of Jiangnan in 1684, and again Zhang Ran was in charge of the rockwork. On its completion, Kangxi transferred his "office" to this garden from the Southern Sea

garden within the city; to make government operations more convenient, former privately owned gardens in the area were taken over as residences for senior officials and for members of the imperial family, who were now closely involved in government, unlike the situation under the Ming. The Kangxi Emperor took an interest in stocking the garden with exotic birds in cages, including wild geese from the north, crested white ducks, peacocks, and parrots, while he noted that the plants included "peony and white lilac, wild plum, flowering peach and magnolia, and acres of vines brought from Hami [in Turkestan]."[24]

Once the Yongzheng Emperor (1678–1735, r. 1722–1735) had succeeded his father Kangxi, he transferred the Garden of Expansive Springtime to his mother, the Dowager Empress, and it continued to house the Dowager Empresses and the other widows of the previous emperors during the following Qianlong and Jiaqing (1796–1820) reigns.

Fig. 149 *Absorbing the Ancient and Containing the Modern* (detail)

Shen Yuan (fl. 18th century) and Tang Dai (1673–after 1752) Album leaf from *Forty Views of the Garden of Perfect Brightness*

This shows one of the complexes of buildings within the Garden of Perfect Brightness. Although the garden is best known for its European buildings (see fig. 150 on page 126), the great majority of its buildings were in Chinese style. The "view" of this group of buildings in its landscape setting was one of those created by the Yongzheng Emperor. The four character name of the site (in Chinese *Rugu hanjin*) is typical of Qing imperial garden features, whereas it was most usual for garden features to have two- or three-character names.

Fig. 148 The entrance to the Garden of Expansive Springtime, from *The Splendid Rites of Myriad Years of Life* (*Wanshou shengdian*), published by the imperial palace to celebrate the sixtieth birthday of the Kangxi Emperor in 1713. The woodblock-printed illustrations are based on paintings by court artists.
(Library of Congress)

The Garden of Perfect Brightness (*Yuanming Yuan*)

The Garden of Perfect Brightness, often known in English as the Old Summer Palace even though this was not its actual function, lay north of the Garden of Expansive Springtime. It had been granted to Kangxi's heir, the Yongzheng Emperor, before he came to the throne, and he continued to use it as his principal residence once he became emperor. He then enlarged it, only for it to be reconstructed on a grand scale by his son and successor the Qianlong Emperor, who also took up residence there and greatly increased the density of buildings. Yongzheng had included a "farm" in the garden to demonstrate his concern for the prosperity of agriculture and the farmers who formed the great majority of China's population. Qianlong added a number of other rural or agricultural scenes for the same reason.

In the mid-1740s Qianlong had two court artists paint an album of the "Forty Views" of the garden (fig. 149), supposedly to mark its completion. But the emperor never stopped

海晏堂西面十

adding to his garden, and in the 1760s he ordered the construction within it of the Garden of Pacified Waves (*Anlan yuan*), a replica of a private garden in Haining, near Hangzhou, where he had stayed four times on his southern tours. The name alluded to serious flooding on the coast, which he had witnessed on one of these tours; as with the construction of "agricultural" scenes, the emperor, in his pleasure garden, wished to emphasize his concern for his subjects' welfare. Here again we see how a literati garden influenced the design of part of an imperial garden, while imperial patronage also contributed to the expansion and remodeling of the original private garden which had inspired the Garden of Pacified Waves. In the end, in fact,

Fig. 150 "Calm Sea Hall" from *Twenty Views of the European Palaces of the Yuanming Yuan* (1783–86)

Yilantai (fl. 1749–1786)
Copperplate engraving
Height 51.4 cm, width 88.3 cm

This set of copperplate engravings showing the European-style buildings in the Garden of Perfect Brightness was commissioned by the Qianlong Emperor and designed by Yilantai, a Manchu court artist who had been trained in European artistic techniques by the Italian Jesuit court painter Giuseppe Castiglione. The bronze figures of the twelve zodiac animals which can be seen here on either side of the central fountain were looted in 1860 and mostly taken to France; some have now been returned to China.

Fig. 151 Surviving remains of the "Grand Fountains" (*Da shuifa*) building, Garden of Perfect Brightness, Beijing.

there were no less than five reproductions of Jiangnan gardens in one section of the Garden of Perfect Brightness alone.

In pursuit of his self-image as a universal ruler and his craving for novelty, the Qianlong Emperor commissioned the Jesuit missionaries who had gained employment as court artists to design the "European Palaces" (*Xiyang lou*), a group of buildings in baroque European style (fig. 150), constructed between 1747 and 1759, which occupied a small area in the north-east of the park. Since they were built in stone, unlike traditional Chinese timber and brick construction, they were almost the only parts of the Garden of Perfect Brightness to survive the conflagration when it was burnt and looted by British and French forces in 1860, during the Second Opium War, the commanders' idea being to destroy the emperor's personal property rather than let their troops loose in the city of Beijing (fig. 151).

As the Garden of Perfect Brightness was such an important imperial residence during the early to mid-Qing, the Qing archives contain much information about its operation, even down to the number of brooms and dustpans required to clean each building. There were strict rules to regulate the activities of the large staff of gardeners, construction workers, cooks, personal servants, security guards, and others needed to keep the garden running smoothly.

Fig. 152 *View of Rehe* (1709?)
Leng Mei
Hanging scroll, ink and color on silk
Height 254.8 cm, width 172.5 cm
Palace Museum, Beijing

This synoptic view, by the court artist Leng Mei, of the central and most "garden-like" part of the Mountain Estate for Escaping the Summer Heat shows how the techniques of European perspective have been seamlessly absorbed into what purports to be a traditional Chinese landscape painting.

The Mountain Estate for Escaping the Summer Heat

Away from the Beijing area, the major resort of the early Qing emperors was the Mountain Estate for Escaping the Summer Heat (*Bishu shanzhuang*) in Jehol (Rehe or "Warm River") near the present-day city of Chengde, where construction started in the very early 18th century (fig. 152). This site lay about halfway between Beijing and the great Mulan hunting-grounds to the north. The Mulan hunting-grounds were near the original home territory of the Manchus who had established

Fig. 153 *The Qianlong Emperor Hunting Hare* (1755)

Giuseppe Castiglione and others
Hanging scroll, ink and color on silk
Height 115.5 cm, width 181.4 cm
Palace Museum, Beijing

This painting, in which Castiglione painted the horses and riders while other court artists painted the landscape background, shows the 45-year-old emperor displaying his skill in equestrian archery on one of his favorite horses. As a child, he had practiced this skill in his grandfather Kangxi's Garden of Expansive Springtime.

the Qing dynasty in 1636, prior to their conquest of China in 1644–45. The hunting-grounds were a gift to the Kangxi Emperor from his allies (effectively his subjects) the Mongols, and the Qing used the hunting-grounds to get close, both geographically and diplomatically, to the Mongols, who were vulnerable to pressure from Russia to the north. However, Mulan was too far from the capital to be practical as a regular summer retreat, so Jehol was more suitable. The early Qing emperors from Kangxi to Qianlong, however well-educated they were in the culture of China, felt it was very important to preserve their Manchu heritage, and they generally decamped to the Mountain Estate to spend the summer riding, practicing archery, and hunting (fig. 153).

The Kangxi Emperor evidently loved the site, and put a great deal of thought into beautifying and celebrating it. He designated thirty-six scenic views with names such as "Misty Ripples Bringing Brisk Air" (*Yanbo zhishuang*), "Pine Winds through Myriad Vales" (*Wanhe songfeng*), or "Moon Boat with Cloud Sails" (*Yunfan yuefang*). He personally wrote a poem on each site, with a brief introductory description in prose, and gave orders for two sets of illustrations, one set of woodblock prints by the court artist Shen Yu (1649–after 1728) and one of copperplate engravings by Matteo Ripa (1682–1746), a Jesuit missionary who spent thirteen years employed as a Qing court artist (figs. 154 and 155). Ripa was able to send sets of his engravings back to Europe,

Fig. 154 "Morning Glow on the Western Ridge" (*Xiling chenxia*)

Shen Yu
Woodblock print

The building which formed the central point in the eleventh of the Kangxi Emperor's "Thirty-Six Views" could be entered from a corridor at ground level. Once inside, the visitor would discover stairs leading to a lower floor by the water's edge.

and also kept a detailed journal of his experiences. These images—the first eye-witness depictions of a Chinese garden ever seen in Europe—and the writings of other Jesuits about the Qing imperial gardens gave rise to another aspect of the social history of Chinese gardens: their role in radically altering landscape gardening in Europe in the 18th century, from the formal style seen at palaces such as Versailles to the so-called *jardin anglo-chinois* ("Anglo-Chinese garden") associated with designers such as Lancelot "Capability" Brown (1716–1783).

The Qing emperors also used the Mountain Estate as a theater of diplomatic activity, receiving delegations from

Fig. 155 "Morning Glow on the Western Ridge"(*Xiling chenxia*) (1711–13)

Matteo Ripa
Copperplate engraving
Height 45 cm, width 28 cm
Palace Museum, Taibei

Matteo Ripa's comment in Italian on this "view" describes the building as a "lodge for recreation" (*casino di recreazione*), adding that such buildings in the Mountain Estate were intended simply for beauty and ornament, and as places to take the air.

other lands, including Lord Macartney's unsuccessful embassy from George III of Britain in 1793. Envoys would often be received in felt tents or yurts, in a nod to Mongol customs. To impress visitors from Tibet and central or inner Asia, the Qianlong Emperor, who saw himself as a Buddhist universal ruler (a *cakravartin* or "wheel-turning ruler"), constructed a number of Lama-Buddhist temples (fig. 156), though these were more theatrical scenery than religious institutions.

It is clear that, compared to the Ming emperors, the Qing emperors had a completely different attitude towards their parks or pleasure grounds. The Qing emperors—at least the early ones, who were most closely in touch with their Manchu heritage—seem to have found it enjoyable, even essential, to move out of the Forbidden City into their garden residences, whether close to the capital or further afield. Officials of the central government were expected to follow the emperor rather than remain in the ministries in Beijing, so the parks outside the city and at the Mountain Estate were provided with office

Fig. 156 This Lama-Buddhist temple in the Mountain Estate for Escaping the Summer Heat was built in a mixture of Han-Chinese and Tibetan styles to mark the visit of the Third Panchen Lama in 1781 on the occasion of the Qianlong Emperor's seventieth birthday.

buildings, and presumably living quarters as well, for large numbers of officials. The Qing emperors' mobility may well have been connected to their ethnic heritage: although not a nomadic people, the Manchus had traditionally lived by hunting and fishing rather than settled agriculture, and were therefore accustomed to moving around in pursuit of seasonal game. As the Kangxi Emperor noted, "It is when one is beyond the Great Wall that the air and soil refresh the spirit: one leaves the beaten road and strikes out into untamed country; … instead of feeling hemmed in, there is a sense of freedom."[25] The Ming rulers, coming from the Han-Chinese tradition of settled agriculture going back millennia, had preferred to remain in one place, or at most to make occasional excursions out of their capital city to the suburban area.

Princely Gardens—Prince Gong's Mansion

The Qing did not follow the Ming practice of effectively banishing sons of the emperor from the capital (and as a result, some emperors had to deal with considerable problems of conflict between their sons). There were therefore a number of princely gardens in Beijing. Usually these were not owned in perpetuity by the family of a particular prince, but were granted by the emperor to the prince for use during his lifetime, reverting to imperial ownership on the prince's death. A surviving example is the garden of Prince Gong's Mansion (*Gongwang fu*) which was situated inside the western wall of Beijing. This garden was originally constructed in 1777 for the Manchu official Heshen (1750–1799), who was highly favored by the Qianlong Emperor. In emulation of the European Palaces in the Garden of Perfect Brightness, Heshen had various European-style constructions added to his gardens, including a gateway still to be seen in the garden of Prince Gong's Mansion (fig. 157). Heshen is said to have been so corrupt and avaricious that his property on his death was worth over one billion taels of silver (one tael [Chinese *liang*] is about 38 grams or one and one-third ounces). All this property was confiscated and his garden was granted to the youngest son of the Qianlong Emperor. Later, in 1852, the Xianfeng Emperor (1831–1861, r. 1850–1861) gave the garden to his brother Prince Gong (Aisingioro Yixin, 1833–1898), who became a prominent statesman and diplomat of the late Qing (fig. 158). The current layout of the (much restored) garden probably dates from the early 1870s. After the end of the Qing dynasty, the mansion with its garden became the property of the Catholic Benedictine order, who used it as the campus of Fu Jen (Furen) Catholic University; the university inaugurated the academic journal *Monumenta Serica*, still one of the leading

Fig. 157   The European-style gate in the garden of Prince Gong's Mansion, originally built for the 18th-century court official Heshen.

Fig. 158   Photograph of Prince Gong at leisure in his garden (1872)

John Thomson (1837–1921)

The Scottish photographer John Thomson lived in Hong Kong from 1868 to 1872, travelling widely in China and taking a great variety of photographs. The fact that the statesman Prince Gong agreed to sit for this very informal portrait shows he understood how he could use his garden for self-representation in a new way, projecting his image, through the novel technology of photography, to an international audience.

sinological journals though now published in Germany. It seems appropriate that the former garden residence of the diplomat Prince Gong should be linked to a publication which continues to promote deeper international understanding of China.

CHAPTER TEN
PRIVATE GARDENS IN THE QING DYNASTY

In the early Qing dynasty, the style of literati gardens remained much the same as in the late Ming, but later in the Qing, garden style changed, as did many other aspects of art and culture. The pursuit of simplicity and restraint characteristic of the late-Ming literati weakened and was replaced by a more elaborate and extravagant esthetic, possibly influenced by Manchu cultural preferences. At the same time, as noted in Chapter Nine, the distinction between literati, merchant, and imperial gardens became blurred, with each type of garden now influencing the style of the others (fig. 159). The social division between literati and merchants itself started to disappear, as more merchant families aspired to official status, while literati or scholar-official families found it increasingly acceptable as well as necessary

to become involved in trade as a way of ensuring an income in deteriorating socio-economic conditions. Towards the end of the dynasty, many officials came to believe that the adoption of modern industrial methods was the only way that China could hold her own against Western economic and military might, and state involvement in industry—on

Fig. 159 *The East Garden* (1710; detail)
Yuan Jiang (fl. 1680–1730)
Ink and color on silk
Dimensions of the complete handscroll: height 59.8 cm, length 370.8 cm
Shanghai Museum

The grand East Garden in Yangzhou, belonging to someone named Qiao Yu who was probably a merchant, was much admired by some well-known literati of the time, whose detailed descriptions of the garden quite closely match this depiction by Yuan Jiang, an artist who specialized in architectural scenes.

a much grander scale than the traditional government monopolies on salt and iron or the imperial household's production of handicrafts for palace use—further broke down the boundaries between the activities of merchants and officials.

As a result, it becomes hard to see any clear distinction, in gardens surviving from the late Qing, between those belonging to literati and those belonging to merchants. Some wealthy merchants were able to create gardens on a grand scale, such as the great gardens of Yangzhou (fig. 160), but at the other end of the scale, we have a glimpse from the early Qing of a very small garden behind the shop of an apothecary in Shaoxing, Zhejiang Province, used partly for the cultivation of medicinal herbs, which was shaded by trees and adorned by flowers in season. Although its owner Lu Yungu (d. 1670) was uneducated, he was a natural connoisseur of the arts, and in his garden, "Beside a low wall beyond the window, a row of small-scale scenes in basin-ponds had been arrayed; so neatly arranged were their trees

Fig. 160 The Ge Garden (Bamboo Garden) in Yangzhou is one of the great merchant gardens of the late Qing.

and rocks that they embodied the painterly qualities of masterpieces by the Yuan dynasty artists Ni Zan or Huang Gongwang."[26]

During the early to mid-Qing, many literati, whether or not they held official positions, were co-opted into working on a wide range of imperially-sponsored publications, large-scale projects for which the Qing dynasty was noted. Often these imperial scholarly activities were carried out in private literati gardens, further blurring the

distinction between imperial and private gardens. For example, the scholar-official and bibliophile Xu Qianxue (1631–1694) worked as editor of both the official *Ming History* and the *Comprehensive Gazetteer of the Great Qing*, establishing the project offices, staffed by numerous literati, in various private gardens situated on the Dongting Hills of Lake Tai near Suzhou (fig. 161). One of these gardens, named the Garden that Borders upon Greenness (*Yilü yuan*), had been designed, as Xu records, by Zhang Ran, the son of Zhang Lian (see Chapters Eight and Eleven).

Fig. 161   This view over the Eastern Dongting Hill on Lake Tai suggests the peaceful landscape environment in which Xu Qianxue and his colleagues undertook work on the massive projects of compiling the *Ming History* and the *Comprehensive Gazetteer of the Great Qing*.

Gardens as Feminine Spaces

Another interesting social change, already referred to in Chapter Seven, is a noticeable transition in the very late Ming or early Qing from the garden being regarded as primarily a masculine space, where men held scholarly gatherings and carried out typically male activities often related to their social roles as scholar-officials, to a conception of the garden as a realm associated primarily with femininity. This may have been partly because in the early Qing many literati withdrew into the private sphere out of loyalty to the Ming and reluctance to serve the new regime: the private sphere of home, family, and garden naturally had a much greater feminine component than the world of government service. (However, why do we see no evidence of "feminization" of the garden in the Yuan dynasty, when literati loyal to the Song were in a comparable position?)

The stereotypical "beautiful woman" (*meiren*) as a subject in art is identified with the space of the garden in a literary work entitled *Delight in Adornment* by a late Ming—early Qing author, Wei Yong (fl. 1643–1654), who describes the ideal setting for such a beauty in an elegant garden residence: "Outside, one should find winding balustrades along crooked paths and rare flowers that reflect one another, filling up all the space. The place can never be complete if potted flowers and miniature landscapes are absent. [Such arrangements are necessary] because a beauty is a flower's 'true self' and a flower captures a beauty's

momentary image."[27] The identification of beautiful women with flowers is certainly not new, but the feminization of the garden is (fig. 162). In the early Qing, moreover, there appeared a fashion for manuals or catalogues of the activities and accouterments of "beauties." The activities are often related to gardens: "taking care of orchids," "watching flowers on a spring morning," "studying painting by copying the shadows of orchid and bamboo."[28] At much the same time, the representation of "beauties" in art, particularly court art, became standardized in groups of twelve images, often corresponding to the twelve months of the year, indicated by different seasonal flowers; in these images the illusionistic effect of their setting seems to be as important as the representation of the women themselves (fig. 163). It is noticeable that these beauties are not individualized at all: we have here an extreme example of the "male gaze," an identification of generic women with generic gardens which presumably has

Above

Fig. 163 *Paintings of Ladies: Reciting Poetry in Wind and Rain*
Jiao Bingzhen (fl. 1689–1726)
Ink, color, and gold on silk
Height 30.9 cm, width 20.4 cm
Palace Museum, Taibei

Jiao Bingzhen was a Qing court painter. This album leaf of "beauties" carrying out a standard activity of poetry recitation in a garden setting shows the influence of Western linear perspective, which Jiao probably learnt from European colleagues while employed in the imperial observatory. Rather than making the garden more "real," it seems to enhance its illusory and mysterious nature.

Below

Fig. 162 *Women Enjoying the Spring Festival* (1636)
Huang Juan (fl. 1630–1656)
Handscroll, ink and color on silk
Height 38 cm, length 311.2 cm
Shanghai Museum

Groups of beautiful ladies, accompanied by their maidservants, enjoy the spring scene, with trees in blossom and willows newly in leaf. Some are seated in pavilions, while others picnic in the open air or admire the scenery. No men appear here: even the boat is rowed by a maidservant. The handscroll format allows the viewer to share the women's movement through the space of the garden.

very little to do with the actual experience of real gardens by real women.

The image of women in gardens during the Qing owes much to the great 18th-century novel *The Dream of the Red Chamber* (*Honglou meng*), also known as *The Story of the Stone* (*Shitou ji*), in which the garden of the Jia family is presented as a "lyric enclave" in which the young women of the family and their spoilt cousin, the hero Jia Baoyu, lead a charmed life of poetic and artistic activities, although eventually the decline and fall of the family is paralleled by the garden's deterioration. The detailed descriptions of the idyllic life of these privileged young people (fig. 164) led to a fashion among young women in the later Qing dynasty of emulating their activities in the garden. The garden is also a feminine space in the sense that it is created to celebrate a visit home by a daughter of the Jia family who has had the high honor of being chosen as an imperial consort, and it is she who gives the garden its name of Prospect Garden (*Daguan yuan*) and also names many of the garden's pavilions and other features.

The idea of young women leading literary lives in a garden was not just fictional, however. The Banana Garden poetry club

Fig. 164 A Qing-dynasty illustration to *The Dream of the Red Chamber*, showing the life and activities of the young women in Prospect Garden. Female readers were particularly inspired by the detailed descriptions of the young women's lives, especially the heroine Lin Daiyu's romantic action of burying fallen flowers, foretelling her own tragic fate in dying young.

was founded in Hangzhou in the 17th century by a gentrywoman for her female relatives and friends, and continued from the 1660s to the 1680s. The women of this small group were not mere dilettanti but serious and well-respected poets. Shang Jinglan (see Chapter Seven), from nearby Shaoxing, praised the literary ability of one of the poets, who died young, and their poetry was also admired by male critics. A poem by one of their number, Qian Fenglun (1644–1703), describes the setting of a winter gathering of the group: "Shrubs and flowers wither in severe frost, / Heavy dewdrops evaporate in the dawn sun." Another of her poems gives a vivid picture of the plants after which the club was named: "The greening banana leaves, / The reddening peony flowers, / In wild profusion rival each other in lush beauty."[29] The exact location of the Banana Garden (*Jiao yuan*) has not been identified, but it may well have been one of the private gardens situated beside

Hangzhou's West Lake, which is referred to in the latter poem. As with the activities of gentrywomen in gardens in the late Ming which paralleled those of elite men, the Banana Garden poets were creating a female equivalent to the male poetry societies which met in the gardens of their participants. As well as poetry, the women of the Banana Garden club took an interest in fiction and drama, and three of them contributed to a famous commentary, written entirely by women, on the Ming drama set in a garden, *The Peony Pavilion*, with whose heroine they identified or sympathized.

Somewhat later, in Nanjing, the male writer Yuan Mei (1716–1798) became notorious for teaching a group of female students of poetry in his Garden of Accommodation (*Suiyuan*) (fig. 165). It was thought improper for a man to teach—or indeed have any contact with—young ladies who were not members of his family, but Yuan Mei and the students' relatives ignored the lurid imaginings of censorious neighbors and the lessons continued. Yuan Mei published some of his students' work

under the title *Selected Poems by the Female Disciples of the Garden of Accommodation* (*Suiyuan nüdizi shixuan*). Again we see women of elite families acting in ways that almost exactly paralleled those of their male relatives, who might also gather around a well-known teacher of literary art. Yuan Mei's garden had belonged to Cao Yin (1658–1712), who was close to the Kangxi Emperor and hosted him in the garden on his imperial tours in south China. Cao Yin was the grandfather of Cao Xueqin (1715–1763), the author of *The Dream of the Red Chamber* (see fig. 164), and Yuan Mei believed that his garden had inspired the novel's Prospect Garden.

From the late 18th or early 19th century we have a memoir, *Six Records of a Floating Life* (*Fusheng liuji*), written by an unsuccessful and impoverished literatus named Shen Fu (1763–c. 1810), which tells us about his life with his beloved wife Chen Yun. Although the couple both loved gardens, they never had enough money to acquire a garden of their own, but they enjoyed visiting other gardens, cultivating pot-plants, and appreciating flowers. On one occasion Yun dressed up as a man in order to accompany her husband to a temple festival which involved a flower-arranging competition. The disguise was successful at first, and Yun was able to walk around and look at the different flower displays, but then they came across the daughters of one of the festival organizers, sitting concealed behind their family's flower display (as women they were not permitted to move around among the visitors). Yun forgot her role, started chatting, and put her hand on the shoulder of one of the girls: this breach of etiquette was so shocking that she had to confess immediately that she was a woman herself! Fortunately everyone took it as a great joke.

Fig. 165   A woodblock-printed image of Yuan Mei's Garden of Accommodation

This was the garden in which Yuan Mei taught his female students the art of literary composition. When Yuan Mei bought the abandoned garden in 1748 it was known as the Sui Garden because it had belonged to a family named Sui; Yuan changed the character *sui* to one meaning "to suit" because he had the garden designed to suit or accommodate the lie of the land.

Gardens in Yangzhou

During the Qing dynasty, some cities came to be particularly associated with gardens, notably Yangzhou. Yangzhou reached its peak as a city of gardens in the mid-Qing. According to a late 18th century book which gives a detailed description of the city, *The Painted Barges of Yangzhou* by Li Dou (1749–1817), while Hangzhou was famous for its landscape and Suzhou for its commercial activity (see fig. 147 on page 123), Yangzhou was most famous for its gardens. This is certainly a contrast to the modern perception of Suzhou as the garden city *par excellence*. Many if not most of the Yangzhou gardens were owned by the wealthy salt-merchants, often from the Huizhou region, who settled in the city because of its position as a vital transport node at the junction of the Yangtze River and the Grand Canal. Yangzhou gardens became particularly known for their rockery work. Yangzhou was some distance from Lake Tai, the source of the most valued garden rocks, as well as from other sources of rocks such as Anhui and Jiangxi; fine rocks were therefore expensive. The use of such rocks, and the greater variety of rocks used compared to gardens in Suzhou and Hangzhou, is a sign of the wealth of those who created the gardens of Yangzhou. Salt-merchants did have a great advantage in acquiring rocks from elsewhere, since the barges which transported their salt from Yangzhou all over the Jiangnan region could be used on their return journey to transport rocks to Yangzhou, thus avoiding the additional cost of relocation.

The use of a variety of rocks can be seen particularly clearly in one of Yangzhou's surviving gardens, the Ge Garden (*Geyuan*, which can be translated as Bamboo Garden), created on the site of an older garden by a leading salt-merchant in the early 19th century, though it has been substantially renovated

Fig. 166   The "summer mountain" in the Ge Garden, Yangzhou, Jiangsu Province

This part of the garden uses the contorted, foraminous Lake Tai rocks to create a light and airy grotto landscape with cooling water to counteract the summer heat.

since then. The garden is divided into four sections, each representing one of the four seasons, and different types of rocks are used to suggest the season: thus reddish-brown *huangshi* rocks are used to echo red autumnal foliage in the "autumn" section, and white *xuan* rocks recall snow-covered mountains in the "winter" section, where the flat ground also has crazy paving to suggest cracking ice. "Spring" is represented by the tall, thin "bamboo-shoot" rocks set among bamboo near the entrance (see fig. 160 on page 133), while in the "summer" section, Lake Tai rocks form an artificial cavern or grotto with water flowing through it to provide coolness in the summer heat (fig. 166). The garden owner would certainly impress his guests by entertaining them in such a comfortable environment.

Yangzhou gardens reached a height of splendor during the 18th-century reign of the Qianlong Emperor, when his frequent imperial tours of the Jiangnan region meant that he always passed through the transportation node of Yangzhou. The imperial visits stimulated the wealthy residents of Yangzhou to develop splendid gardens in which the emperor could be entertained (fig. 167). Their wealth allowed the use of costly materials in the construction of their gardens and the associated buildings: not just splendid rocks but also marble paving and rare woods such as *nanmu* or *zitan* for interior woodwork. An imperial visit would naturally give a garden owner almost unimaginable prestige, so it is not surprising that those garden owners on whom the emperor bestowed examples of his poetry and calligraphy had these proudly displayed as inscriptions in their gardens.

There is evidence of a vogue at this time for the novel and spectacular in Yangzhou merchant gardens. The imperial style of garden buildings was emulated here, resulting in more elaborate structures, often of more than one storey. This may have been due to the presence in Yangzhou not only of craftsmen from the north who were familiar with the architecture of the imperial palaces, but also of craftsmen from Huizhou employed by the Huizhou merchants: buildings of two or three storeys were more common in Huizhou than in most other parts of China, owing to the paucity of flat land and the relative abundance of timber from the mountain forests. We also hear of the installation of features such as waterfalls and fountains, perhaps inspired by the water-features designed by the Jesuits in the imperial gardens of Beijing (see Chapter Nine). This suggests a growing similarity between imperial and merchant tastes in garden design, while literati style perhaps remained more restrained. This similarity may have been further underpinned by the liminal status of Yangzhou, situated on the north bank of the Yangtze and therefore not technically part of Jiangnan yet very close to that region, making it a city whose culture combined elements from both north and south.

To impress the emperor, the wealthy merchants of Yangzhou also developed the river landscape to the west and north-west of the walled city by extending the gardens already there and combining them into a designed landscape which was effectively a public pleasure-ground. Previously named Baozhang Lake, the area became known as Slender West Lake because of its perceived

Fig. 167 "Mist and Rain over the Four Bridges," a woodblock illustration to Li Dou's *The Painted Barges of Yangzhou*, which describes many of the 17th and 18th century gardens of Yangzhou. The "four bridges" were in a garden belonging to the Huizhou salt merchant Huang Lüxian; the Qianlong Emperor wrote a poem about this garden on his fourth visit to Yangzhou in 1765. The garden was in the Baozhang Lake or Slender West Lake area to the north-west of Yangzhou city: its famous "Five Pavilion Bridge" can be seen in the background.

resemblance to Hangzhou's celebrated West Lake. There is evidence, too, that at this time some garden owners used part of their land to produce plants for sale, thus developing commercial activities within their gardens. At the same time, not only semi-public institutions such as academies and guild-halls, but purely commercial establishments such as restaurants, brothels, and bath-houses were felt to be incomplete without something in the way of a garden.

Already in the Northern Song dynasty, Yangzhou was as famous for its herbaceous peonies (*Paeonia lactiflora*; Chinese *shaoyao*) as Luoyang was for its tree-peonies (*P. suffruticosa* or *P. moutan*; Chinese *mudan*). Both these types of flowers were widely admired in the Song dynasty, but by the Ming dynasty the herbaceous peony was regarded as inferior to the tree-peony, and its association with wealth and splendor meant that it did not fit the preference for simplicity and restraint in literati esthetics. The continuing popularity

Fig. 168   Herbaceous peony, a flower which appears in many varieties and colors. Yangzhou was noted for its peonies, which remained popular throughout the Qing dynasty. (photo by author)

Fig. 169   **Stage building in the He Family Garden, Yangzhou, Jiangsu Province**

This miniature theatre is set in a rectangular pond: the flat surface of the water enables the sound to carry more effectively to the audience sitting around the courtyard. The upper story of the two-story building which surrounds the courtyard allowed the women of the family and their friends to enjoy the performance also, without coming in contact with the male guests on the ground floor.

of herbaceous peonies in Yangzhou through the Qing dynasty may reflect the prevalence of a mercantile esthetic there (fig. 168).

By the late 19th century, the distinction between merchant and literatus had become so blurred as to be largely meaningless. Both roles were combined in the owner of one Yangzhou garden which survives from this time: the *Jixiao shanzhuang* (literally "Mountain Villa for Expressing One's Feelings in Whistling," alluding to a Daoist practice), usually called the He Family Garden (*He yuan*). It was constructed by He Weijian (better known as He Zhidao, 1835–1908), a member of a scholar-official family from Anhui, who chose to retire to Yangzhou in 1883 rather than take his chances in the unstable conditions of rural Anhui. Some years later, he helped his nephews to set up an industrial enterprise in the booming commercial city of Shanghai and soon afterwards moved there himself. He was only one of a number of late-Qing officials who were also involved in commerce and industry, which they saw as a way to strengthen China in its then weak international position. During the years when He Zhidao lived in his Yangzhou garden residence, he had a stage building constructed to entertain his family and guests with theatrical performances (fig. 169). As we saw in Chapter Five, it was not unusual to have theatrical performances in private homes during the Ming, but it was only later in the Qing dynasty that purpose-built stage buildings were installed in the homes of the wealthy. In the course of his official duties, He Zhidao had spent some time at the Qing-dynasty Chinese embassy in Paris, and some architectural features in the garden show signs of European influence.

Gardens of Tianjin Merchants

Major commercial cities beyond Jiangnan also became noted during the Qing dynasty for impressive merchant gardens. Tianjin in the north, which served as the seaport for Beijing, was, like Yangzhou, a center of the salt trade, as well as producing salt from nearby salt-pans. Since success in the salt trade at this time depended as much, if not more, on political patronage as on economic factors, the salt-merchants of Tianjin had an advantage over others in being located close to the seat of government in Beijing. The Tianjin salt-merchants developed lavish gardens—more than twenty are recorded for the Qing dynasty—which they seem to have based on the literati style and to have used as sites where they could interact with local scholars and officials (fig. 170). Many of these gardens were created along the Haihe River on which Tianjin is situated.

In the early part of the Qing dynasty, the Tianjin merchants' gardens appear to have been relatively small, and therefore they made much use of "borrowed views," particularly of the riverscape, to increase the sense of space within the garden. In other respects also, these merchant garden owners followed literati

Fig. 170 *Reading in the Night Rain in the Autumn Manor*
Zhu Min
Tianjin Museum
The painting depicts the scenery of the Manor West of the Water (*Shuixi zhuang*) belonging to the Tianjin salt merchant Zha Riqian (1667–1741).

esthetics, constructing garden buildings in rustic materials such as bamboo and thatch. They took part in typical literati cultural activities such as "elegant gatherings" where the participants wrote poems which might later be published in a collection commemorating the occasion, and used their gardens to display their collections of art and antiques.

During the 18th century, as the expansive Qing empire undertook costly wars in central Asia, the merchants' financial contributions to the government gained them official titles, enabling them to raise their social status further. Now they wanted to make their gardens more conspicuous by constructing them closer to, or even within, the city. Their wealth enabled them to buy up prime waterfront real estate, and to increase the size of their gardens, while construction within the gardens became more elaborate. In these splendid gardens, the parties and entertainments offered to distinguished locals and visitors became ever grander. However, economic and social decline in the later Qing dynasty led to a decline in the salt-merchants' wealth and to the concomitant neglect and dilapidation of many of their gardens, especially those which had been used primarily for entertainment rather than as regular dwellings. As a result, the wealthier merchants withdrew within their garden compounds where they lived still in considerable luxury but without the extravagant social activities of earlier and more prosperous times.

Gardens of Guangdong

Another great commercial port city, with its own distinctive garden tradition, was Guangzhou in the far south. Guangzhou had been a foreign trade port frequented by merchants from afar ever since the Tang dynasty, when its historic mosque was founded for the use of visiting or resident Arab merchants, possibly as early as the 7th century. It was in the 18th century, however, that Guangzhou was designated by the Qing government as the only port through which Europeans and North Americans could trade with China. A group of wealthy local merchants, known as the Hong merchants or the Co-hong, was designated as the intermediary for the westerners for the

Fig. 171   This "export painting" by an anonymous Chinese artist almost certainly shows a part of one of the Pan family's gardens, the Garden of Six Pines (*Liusong yuan*), as the horizontal board on the central pavilion bears the name "Six Pines Pavilion" (*Liusong ting*). The composition is duplicated in other export paintings, which were sold to foreign traders in Guangzhou as souvenirs to take home. (British Library, London)

duration of this "Canton system" of trade (named after the old European name for Guangzhou or Guangdong), until the Opium Wars of the mid-19th century led to the opening up to foreign trade of other major Chinese ports. The Hong merchants were responsible not only for trade, but for the foreign merchants' living conditions and for their good behavior; thus they became unofficial diplomats as well as traders. As such, they often entertained the foreigners in their garden residences. As a result, though not so much writing in Chinese about the 18th and 19th century gardens survives, we have a surprising amount of evidence about these "Lingnan style" gardens (Lingnan is a traditional name for the region of Guangdong and Guangxi), in the form of written accounts by westerners, paintings and prints by both Chinese and western artists, and early photographs.

Lingnan gardens had a distinctive style, quite different from the style of Beijing in the north, or the Jiangnan gardens of the Yangtze delta region. This is not surprising given the different climatic conditions and vegetation. They were more geometric in layout, particularly as regards ponds within the gardens, which were usually rectangular rather than having a "naturalistic" shape. They were more colorful than Jiangnan gardens, often having red-painted railings and other architectural features. Very noticeable was the practice, which can be seen in almost all surviving painted and photographic images, of having rows of potted plants (not usually miniaturized but full-size plants in pots) displayed on low balustrades made of ceramic tiles alongside paths, buildings, or water features. Potted plants were much

Fig. 172   James Wathen, "Banqueting Room at a Mandarin's House near Canton," aquatint, from Wathen's *Journal of a Voyage, in 1811 and 1812, to Madras and China*

This depiction of part of a garden belonging to Pan Youdu (Pan Khequa II) or his brother Pan Youwei, though somewhat fanciful, is believed to be fairly accurate: Wathen did dine with the Pan family at least once, and the botanist John Reeves, who collected plants in Guangzhou for Kew Gardens during the period 1812–1831, and was friendly with both Pan brothers, described the image as "tolerably correct." The large tree on the left represents one of the banyan trees for which the Pan garden was known.

used in Chinese gardens generally, but this relatively rigid style of display seems to be unique to Lingnan gardens.

Two outstanding Hong merchant families were the Pan and the Wu families (fig. 171). The most notable member of the Wu family was Wu Bingjian (1769–1843), known to the Western merchants as "Howqua" (*Wu guan* or "Official Wu"); he was said to be the richest man on earth in his time. Both families owned gardens on the south bank of the Pearl River, more or less opposite the so-called "Thirteen Factories" (agencies), which included the foreign merchants' residences as well as their offices. The Pan family were particularly hospitable to the foreign merchants, inviting them to banquets in their garden residences and allowing them to meet their children (fig. 172). These moments of inclusion in family life must have been a comfort to the Westerners, who

Fig. 173 *The Garden of Fragrant Shade*
(c. 1850–1875)
Tian Yu
Guangdong Provincial Museum

This garden, situated on the south bank of the Pearl River, south-west of Guangzhou city, was originally known as the "East Garden" (*Dong yuan*) and belonged to the Pan family. It was purchased from them by the equally wealthy Wu family and renamed Garden of Fragrant Shade.

Fig. 174 *Howqua's Garden* (mid-19th century)
Studio of Tingqua (Guan Lianchang, 1809–1870)
Gouache on paper
Peabody Essex Museum

Guan Lianchang, whose studio produced this export painting, came from a family of Western-style painters in Guangzhou. Potted plants can be seen here lined up around the large tree in the foreground and arranged along the balustrade of the embankment in the middle distance. The octagonal pavilion visible through the columns of the hall on the left is the one which can be seen on the zigzag bridge across the pond towards the left of fig. 173; the little pavilion on the bridge in the center of this painting (immediately to the left of the tree-trunk) is just visible to the right of the octagonal pavilion in fig. 173.

were not permitted to have their own families with them. The Pan and Wu families both made use of their gardens to interact with influential local literati and government officials, participating in cultural activities, as did other wealthy merchants in Guangzhou, but the amount of cultural interaction between these two families and the foreign merchants was exceptional.

This interaction extended to the exchange of plants and botanical knowledge between the two sides. This was perhaps made easier by the fact that one of the Wu family's gardens, the Garden of Fragrant Shade (*Fuyin yuan*; fig. 173), was located in the same area,

Fig. 175 The Mountain Villa of Abundant Shade in Panyu, to the south-west of Guangzhou, was constructed in the 1860s by a wealthy merchant family. Note the similarity of the bridge pavilion here to that in fig. 174; it is characteristic of Lingnan garden style.

on the south bank of the Pearl River, as the famous commercial Fa-tee (Huadi) gardens, which had a vast range of plants for sale and were open to foreign visitors. Contemporary photographs and paintings show plants in the Fa-tee gardens in pots lined up in a way that is very similar to the way they were displayed in private gardens such as the Wus' in distinctively Cantonese style (fig. 174).

As tensions increased between foreign and Chinese merchants in the lead-up to the First Opium War, their cultural exchanges became less frequent, and after the end of the Canton system in the mid-19th century, as Guangzhou's prosperity declined, so did its great merchant gardens. Although no complete gardens survive in Guangzhou itself, there are a few still to be seen in surrounding urban centers, including the Mountain Villa of Abundant Shade (*Yuyin shanfang*) in Panyu (fig. 175) and the Could-Be Garden (*Ke yuan*) in Dongguan.

Gardens in and around Shanghai

Other 19th-century commercial centers also became sites of cultural exchange between China and the west. In Nanxun, near Shanghai, Liu Yong (1826–1899), a merchant who made his fortune in silk and later went into salt, developed a garden which shows clear signs of western influence, the Lesser Lotus Manor (*Xiaolianzhuang*). Construction on the estate began in 1885, though it was not completed until the 1920s. In addition to the "outer" garden, which includes the large lotus pond for which the estate is famous (fig. 176), and the "inner" garden, which

Fig. 176 The Lesser Lotus Manor, Nanxun, Zhejiang Province

The estate, incorporating the famous lotus pond seen here, was named after the "Lotus Blossom Manor" (*Lianhua zhuang*) constructed in nearby Huzhou by the Yuan-dynasty scholar-official Zhao Mengfu (see Chapter Four); this shows the merchant owner Liu Yong's desire to align himself with literati culture.

was more private, the property includes an ancestral temple and the headquarters of the family trust set up to maintain the temple and clan school. In front of the temple are two ceremonial arches, one of which was awarded to Liu Yong by the Guangxu Emperor (1871–1908, r. 1875–1908) for his contribution to flood relief in 1889. This honor is indicative of the very important role played by merchants in public life by this time. The Liu family were clearly eager to display their cultural credentials as well as their wealth and philanthropy: the outer garden includes an open corridor containing calligraphic inscriptions, including one by a famous 18th-century official and calligrapher also named Liu Yong (though with a slightly different *yong* character). As well as showcasing traditional Chinese culture, the Liu family also used the garden to demonstrate their familiarity with Western culture: at the eastern end of the embankment along the north side of the lotus pond stands a brick-built European-style arched gateway, while at the south-west corner of the pond is a two-storey building in French architectural style.

After the so-called Treaty Ports were opened up in the wake of the Opium Wars in the mid-19th century, Shanghai's pivotal position on the Huangpu River near the estuary of the Yangtze, which provides a navigable route reaching far into central and western China, made it the main center of both foreign and Chinese investment and trade. Enormous fortunes were made (and lost) there, and new, culturally mixed ways of life developed. A good example of this

Fig. 177   An old photograph of part of the Aili Garden. The site of the Hardoon Mansion and its garden was cleared in the 1950s to build the Shanghai Exhibition Center.

cultural mix was a garden known as the Aili Garden, attached to the mansion belonging to the wealthy Silas Hardoon (1851–1931), an Iraqi Jewish merchant who made his fortune in Shanghai and married a local woman, Luo Jialing (also known as Liza Roos, 1864–1941), who was a devout Buddhist. Their mansion was built in European style, but the garden (fig. 177), created between 1902 and 1910, was designed in Chinese style by Huang Zongyang (1865–1921), a Buddhist monk who was also an anti-Qing activist. The name of the garden, Aili, represents "love for Li[za]," expressing Hardoon's devotion to his wife.

In prosperous treaty ports such as Shanghai, wealthy Chinese families— particularly those educated in missionary schools or universities, or with overseas connections—often lived in large western-style mansions surrounded by substantial gardens; in order to provide for modern ways of entertaining guests and socializing, these gardens might have extensive lawns (a very un-Chinese garden feature), tennis courts, and other facilities. At the same time, they might also include traditional Chinese components such as rockwork and pavilions. More traditional wealthy families might live in traditional-style buildings, or buildings that were a mixture of traditional and modern arrangements, including traditional courtyard gardens. It could be said that in Shanghai and other treaty ports, a new, hybrid sino-foreign garden style was developing, in which merchants rather than intellectuals were leading the way.

A further development in Shanghai was the creation of gardens with a commercial purpose, such as the Zhang Garden, acquired in 1882 by a man named Zhang Honglu, who worked for the pioneering enterprise the China Merchants Steam Navigation Company (*Zhaoshangju*). The Zhang Garden, constructed in a hybrid Sino-Western style, contained teahouses, restaurants, and entertainment facilities, and charged a fee for access.

Chinese gardens were thus being adapted

to a new style of urban life. Traditionally some semi-public gardens such as temple gardens had provided urban residents with sites for recreation and entertainment (they were often the locations of temple fairs and markets). Now the foreign residents of Shanghai and other treaty ports such as Tianjin and Hankou (Wuhan) introduced the idea of public parks. These first appeared in foreign residential and commercial areas, such as the park on the Bund in Shanghai's International Concession (fig. 178), but as time went on the idea was adopted in Chinese areas also, and now public parks are an accepted part of every Chinese city.

Fig. 178 Public Garden and Bund viewed from Hongkou, Shanghai (c. 1873)

This photograph shows the Public Garden on the Bund newly laid out. The earliest bandstand, seen just to the right of center, was built in 1868 and disappeared after 1874. Although the layout and planting of the gardens looks entirely European (indeed British), this version of the bandstand has the appearance of a Chinese garden pavilion.

CHAPTER ELEVEN
GARDEN DESIGN, HORTICULTURE, AND BOTANY

There is considerable continuity between garden design in the late Ming and the early Qing. The Ming-Qing transition led to great political change but little immediate cultural change, so the style of gardens seems to have remained much the same during the 17th century, and it was only in the 18th century that garden style changed substantially. Thus, some individuals or families seem to have worked as garden designers and creators almost uninterruptedly over the transition period. This was the case for the "Mountain Zhangs" whom we met in Chapter Eight.

Fig. 179 The pagoda on Jade Spring Hill to the north-west of Beijing forms a striking landmark, here seen from across the lake in the Summer Palace. The hill was the site of the imperial Jingming Garden, worked on by Zhang Ran.

The Mountain Zhangs

After the Qing conquest, the court sent for Zhang Lian to come to Beijing to work on the imperial gardens—evidently his fame had spread well beyond his home region—but Zhang Lian refused on the grounds of old age (he would have been in his seventies at least) and sent his youngest son Zhang Ran in his place. Ran worked on part of the Southern Sea garden, particularly the island known as Ocean Terrace (*Yingtai*), the Jingming Garden on Jade Spring Hill (fig. 179), and the Garden of Expansive Springtime (see Chapter Nine). He also designed at least one private garden in Beijing, the Hall of Myriad Willows (*Wanliu tang*) belonging to a high official of the new regime, Feng Pu (1609–1692). The possibility for craftsmen to move between the court and private clients was a new feature of the early Qing dynasty; earlier craftsmen would not have had the option of working for both. This new situation contributed to the mutual influence of imperial and private garden styles in the Qing dynasty (see Chapters Nine and Ten). Zhang Ran's two sons also followed their father's profession, but through their association with the imperial court, their sons were able to obtain official appointments, and so in the fourth generation from Zhang Lian the family returned to the life of the educated elite.

半敩營園

Fig. 180 A woodblock print of the Half-Acre Garden originally designed by Li Yu, from Wanyan Linqing's autobiographical *Tracks of a Wild-Goose in the Snow* (*Hongxue yinyuan tuji*); the book's title alludes to the transience of human life. The enclosing walls of the garden suggest its small size, but it has everything a garden requires: trees, rocks, a pond, bamboo, flowering plants, and an open pavilion from which to enjoy them. As Linqing said of his garden, "I have obtained that which I desired most ardently as a youth with no expectation of success … How very fortunate I am."[30]

Li Yu

The multi-talented late Ming–early Qing entrepreneur Li Yu (also known as Li Liweng, 1610/11–1680) was in a similar situation to his predecessors Zhang Lian and Ji Cheng (see Chapter Eight) as an impoverished literatus needing to earn his keep. A highly enterprising individual, Li Yu found many ways to make a living. He was an accomplished dramatist, who ran his own theater troupe giving public performances. He also wrote fiction, calling his short stories "silent operas," and is perhaps most famous today for his essay collection *Casual Expressions of Idle Feeling* (*Xianqing ouji*), also known as *Random Ventures in Idleness*, which includes extensive material on his views about interior and garden design. He is believed to have designed at least four or five gardens between the late 1640s and the 1670s, including the Half-Acre Garden (*Banmu yuan*) in Beijing (fig. 180). When Wanyan Linqing (1791–1846), a senior official in the first half of the 19th century, acquired this garden, rather than

renaming it, as a new owner would usually do, he kept its original name in order to show his respect for its designer, Li Yu, and thus to identify himself, a Manchu, with the cultural traditions of China.

In *Casual Expressions of Idle Feeling* Li Yu claims two original ideas which do indeed seem to have had an impact on the design of garden buildings. One was the use of a real tree-branch as a window-lattice (fig. 181). Li Yu says the idea came to him after two trees in his garden were submerged in the floods of 1669; too green to be used as firewood, some of their branches, decorated with paper or silk "flowers," were used to frame the window and form the lattice. Li Yu, who was a generation younger than Ji Cheng, certainly

Fig. 181 Window with prunus-branch frame and lattice, as designed by Li Yu.

Fig. 182 This woodblock illustration from Li Yu's *Casual Expressions of Idle Feeling* depicts Li's original idea for a houseboat in which he could drift about on the West Lake, observing the scenery through fan-shaped windows on either side of the cabin, so that it would form a constantly changing "natural painting." Sadly, Li Yu tells us, he was never able to afford such a houseboat, but he put the window idea into effect in his house in Nanjing, to frame the view of Bell Mountain beyond the city.

Fig. 183 "With Whom Shall I Sit?" Pavilion (*Yu shui tong zuo xuan*), Garden of the Artless Administrator, Suzhou, Jiangsu Province

"With whom shall I sit?" comes from a poem by the Song-dynasty poet Su Shi: his answer is "The bright moon, the pure breeze, and myself" (*ming yue, qing feng, wo*). The "pure breeze" could be generated by the fan whose shape this pavilion imitates in its ground plan and also in the form of the window. Such fanciful shapes of pavilions, doors, and windows, which now seem so characteristic of Chinese gardens, started to appear around the time when garden designers such as Ji Cheng and Li Yu were active.

knew of his predecessor's work, as he mentions it in *Casual Expressions of Idle Feeling*, and the flowering prunus branch window design may have been partly inspired by some of Ji Cheng's ideas (see fig. 139 on page 115). Although the use of a real tree-branch in a window might be difficult to replicate, the idea of reproducing a natural branch in wood-carving certainly became widespread. Li Yu's other original creation was a fan-shaped window (fig. 182), which makes the scenery outside appear to the viewer within like a landscape painting on a fan, while to viewers outside, the people within the structure appear like a figure painting. As we saw in Chapter Eight, the use of fanciful shapes for windows and doors, and even for whole buildings, started to appear only in the late Ming. Not only fan-shaped windows, but fan-shaped buildings were placed as features within gardens from this time onwards (fig. 183).

Shitao, Wang Tianyu, and Mushan

We have already seen the prominence of Yangzhou gardens in the Qing dynasty. Li Dou, the late 18th-century historian of Yangzhou, states that the Myriad Rocks Garden (*Wanshi yuan*) of the Yu family in Yangzhou was designed by the artist Shitao (Zhu Ruoji, 1642–1707) who, in addition to his skill at landscape and flower painting, was also skilled at rockery construction. Born in Guilin in south-west China, Shitao was a descendant of the Ming Prince of Jingjiang (see Chapter Six). Like many Ming loyalists in the early Qing, he became a Buddhist monk. He lived mainly in Yangzhou from the 1680s until his death, and is best known as one of the most original painters in the early Qing. However, since the Myriad Rocks Garden was most probably constructed in the 1740s, it is impossible that Shitao was involved with that garden, though it could be that the rockery was a survival from an earlier garden on the same site. A local gazetteer from the very early 19th century (but which may incorporate earlier material) suggests that the rockery in the Myriad Rocks Garden was constructed in accordance with Shitao's landscape painting style by a craftsman named Wang Tianyu, or Wang Tingyu; Wang's descendants still believe that it was he who created the rockery.

The Stone Slab Mountain Villa (*Pianshi shanfang*) in Yangzhou, which was originally a separate garden although it now forms the south-east corner of the He Family Garden (see Chapter Ten), includes a rockery backing against a south-facing wall, of the type which Ji Cheng called a "precipitous mountain," giving the effect of a landscape painting of mountains on the white "paper" of the backing wall. This rockery is also said to have been designed by Shitao. According to an early 19th century source, the garden had "a mound of Lake Tai rocks, fifty or sixty feet high, most remarkable and precipitous; it is said to be the handiwork [literally "the handwriting"] of the Reverend Shitao." This is not contemporary evidence, and indeed there is little to prove the garden's existence before the 18th century, so again it is unlikely that Shitao was actually involved in its design, though it is possible, as in the Myriad Rocks Garden, that the rockery was intended to replicate a Shitao landscape painting. Another early 19th century source attributes the rockery to a monk named Mushan, who has not been securely identified. Nevertheless, when the garden was restored in the 1980s, by which time the rockery was quite dilapidated, Shitao's paintings and his writings on art were used as a guide for its reconstruction (fig. 184).

Ge Yuliang

Towards the end of the 18th century, the Jiangnan region produced another great garden and rockery designer, Ge Yuliang (1764–1830). By this time, the dominant style of rockwork had changed considerably. A more robust economy, as compared to the unstable situation in the early Qing, provided the elite with more disposable income to spend on grand gardens, while advances in technique allowed craftsmen to create more imposing rockeries with quite spacious "caves" within them. These new techniques appear to have developed first in wealthy Jiangnan, but soon spread north, where they can be seen in the imperial gardens of the 18th century, particularly the imperial garden in the north part of the Forbidden City and the Mountain Estate at Jehol (see Chapter Nine).

Ge Yuliang is credited with developing a new method of fitting rocks together without the use of mortar, based on the technique of

Fig. 184   The rockery in the Stone Slab Mountain Villa, although probably not by its reputed designer, the painter Shitao, has been restored according to his artistic style.

Fig. 185   Garden of the Mountain Villa with Embracing Beauty, Suzhou, Jiangsu Pronvince

In 1806–7, the rockery master Ge Yuliang was commissioned to design this garden, believed to be on the site of many previous historic gardens. It is now part of the Suzhou Embroidery Institute. Although the rockery takes up a very small area (about 330 sq. m. within the 1600 sq. m. garden), it is replete with caves, ravines, water-courses, and stairways, giving those who explore it the sense of a much larger mountain.

constructing an arched bridge, so that as the individual rocks settled into place they became ever more stable and firmly fixed. The names of several gardens designed by him are known, but only a few survive. Ge's best-known work today is the rockery in the garden known as the Mountain Villa with Embracing Beauty (*Huanxiu shanzhuang*, which literally means Mountain Villa Surrounded by Flourishing Bamboo) in Suzhou (fig. 185). Constructed in 1806–7 from Lake Tai rocks, this is a remarkably successful example of a highly complex rockery structure situated within a very limited space, yet without any feeling of being cramped or overwhelming in scale. A somewhat similar rockery, almost certainly also the work of Ge Yuliang, can be seen in the Swallow Garden or Swallow Vale Garden (*Yan yuan, Yangu yuan*) in the nearby city of Changshu, dating from around 1825. The garden in Yangzhou known as Xiao Pangu or Little Winding Valley is sometimes attributed to Ge, but it appears that Ge actually worked on another, earlier garden in Yangzhou with the same name: it refers to a famous essay by the Tang prose master Han Yu (768–824), praising the beauty and seclusion of his friend's home in the original Winding Valley. The garden for which Ge was responsible was probably constructed around 1800 but has since disappeared.

The Han Family

The Jiangnan area, and Suzhou in particular, remained a center of highly skilled rockery construction as well as garden design more generally. Han Heng, born in the first half of the 19th century, first brought the Han family to prominence as rockery experts. Three generations of the family became known as the "Mountain Rock Hans" (*Shanshi Han*) and they remained leading rockery craftsmen in Suzhou throughout the 20th century. They contributed significantly to the reconstruction of rockwork in gardens which suffered from the various catastrophes which China has experienced since the 19th century, participating from the 1950s to the 1980s in the restoration of Suzhou gardens including the Garden for Lingering, the Garden of the Artless Administrator, and the Lion Grove. One of three brothers in the third generation, Han Liangshun, was involved in the creation of the Astor Court Chinese garden courtyard in the Metropolitan Museum of Art in New York, completed in 1981.

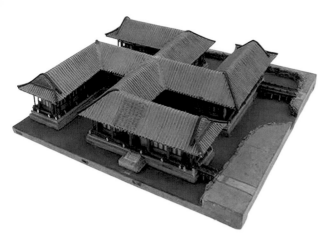

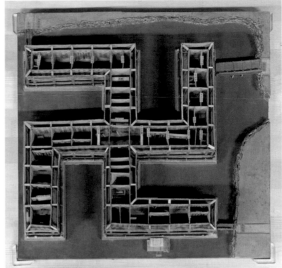

Fig. 186　This swastika-shaped building was originally constructed in 1726–7 as the Yongzheng Emperor's studio named "Peace in All Directions" (*Wanfang anhe*), in the Garden of Perfect Brightness; the model dates from a later restoration project. The swastika was an auspicious Hindu and Buddhist symbol. In Chinese it can stand for the simplified form of the character for 10,000 (*wan* 万), hence the name of the building, which is literally "Peace in Ten Thousand Directions."

Fig. 187　The architectural models made for the Qing emperors by the Lei family could even be disassembled to show the interior structure.

Fig. 188　*Peace in All Directions*
Shen Yuan and Tang Dai
Album leaf from *Forty Views of the Garden of Perfect Brightness*

This painting of part of the Garden of Perfect Brightness shows the environment of the swastika-shaped "Peace in All Directions" studio after its construction was completed.

The "Model Leis"

In the north, a remarkable family of experts in a different branch of the craft of garden creation were the Lei family, known as the "Model Leis" (*Yangshi Lei*). They were construction experts who became specialists in the making of models, particularly of garden architecture, used in the planning and repair of gardens for the Qing imperial family. A number of these models are still extant in the Palace Museum collection (figs. 186–188). The first of seven generations of the family

to be employed by the imperial household was Lei Fada (1619–1693), an experienced builder who had travelled to the capital from the impoverished province of Jiangxi in the 1680s. His son Lei Jinyu also served the Kangxi Emperor, who had such a high regard for him that he joined in celebrating Lei's 70th birthday. Lei's descendants continued to work for the imperial family until the fall of the dynasty in the early 20th century. For a long time, they had a site office in the Garden of Perfect Brightness for convenience of carrying out maintenance and new construction. Three Lei brothers accompanied the Qianlong Emperor on his southern visits in order to reproduce Jiangnan gardens in the imperial parks. The Lei family were primarily builders and interior designers rather than garden craftsmen as such, but they incorporated garden elements into their plans and models.

Fig. 189   Interior view of Chinese greenhouse from *Serres-Chaudes des Chinois* (1777)

Pierre-Martial Cibot
Watercolor on paper
Bibliothèque nationale de France, Paris

In this image, one of the rolled-up mats which could be let down to keep out the cold can be seen at the top of the open door space.

Horticulture and Botany

We have already seen that in very early times, imperial gardens contained hothouses or greenhouses to cultivate plants from warmer climes (see Chapter One). More detailed evidence of the use of greenhouses to raise delicate plants comes from north China in the 18th century: the French Jesuit missionary Pierre-Martial Cibot (1727–1780) wrote on Chinese horticultural techniques and sent back to Paris a number of watercolor paintings (painted either by him or by a Chinese associate), including illustrations of the exterior and interior of a Chinese greenhouse (fig. 189). Cibot arrived in China in 1759 and lived in Beijing for the rest of his life. With a knowledge of natural history, he was interested in Chinese horticultural techniques, and also wrote perceptively about Chinese garden history and esthetics, calling for the adoption of Chinese design principles in European gardens. In the greenhouses which he described, straw mats were suspended outside the floor-to-ceiling paper windows and the door; these could be lowered at

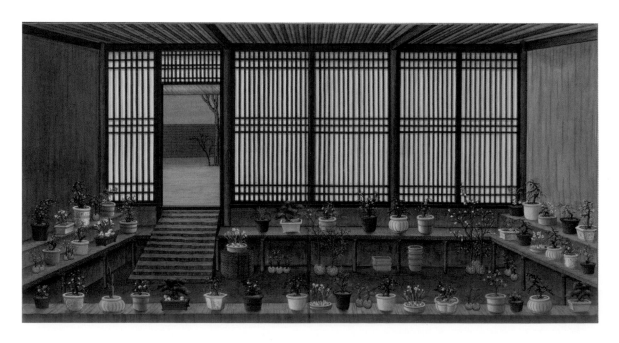

Fig. 190   Persimmon tree, from the 1656 first edition of Boym's *Flora Sinensis*

Biodiversity Heritage Library

The illustration includes the name of the tree in Chinese characters and in transliteration, with the information that "Xu" (*shu*) means "tree" (*arbor* in Latin).

night to keep out the cold and rolled up during the day to let in the sunlight. Some greenhouses were even supplied with heating. At this time the use of greenhouses or hothouses was still a novel technology in Europe, whereas in China they had existed for many centuries.

As contacts between China and the West increased from the 18th century onwards, Europeans and North Americans became aware of the richness of Chinese flora and the Chinese garden tradition. Even in the 17th century, some European visitors to China, with local help, had paved the way to wider knowledge of Chinese flora. A Polish Jesuit, Michael Peter Boym

(c. 1612–1659), wrote the first work in a European language on Chinese plants, with a particular emphasis on their medicinal uses: *Flora Sinensis* (*Chinese Flora*) was published in Vienna in 1656 (fig. 190). Boym accomplished this, undoubtedly with the help of Chinese experts, even while accompanying the court of the last claimant to the Ming throne as he moved around south-west China during all the chaos of the Manchu conquest of that region. A later Jesuit missionary, Pierre Nicolas d'Incarville (1706–1757), even exchanged botanical information with the Qianlong Emperor, and was able to introduce a number of Chinese trees to Europe. He was a gifted amateur, but many Catholic missionaries who actively collected Chinese plants were, like Cibot, trained scientists. Father Armand David (1826–1900) was the first European to observe the "handkerchief tree" (*Davidia involucrata*) which is named after him (fig. 191). The great Swedish botanist Linnaeus (1707–1778) got ships' captains and his former students such as Pehr Osbeck, who travelled to China as chaplain on one of the Swedish East India Company's ships, to bring back botanical specimens

Fig. 191   *Davidia involucrata*, the "handkerchief tree" (sometimes called the dove tree or ghost tree), is named for the striking white bracts which surround the flower.

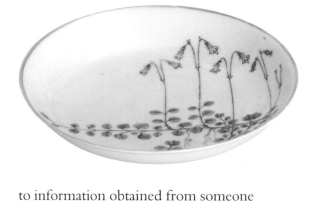

for him (fig. 192); many of the specimens collected by Osbeck are still preserved by the Linnean Society, based in London.

European merchants, too, helped to spread knowledge of China's plants and gardens beyond China's borders. As a young man, the famous British architect Sir William Chambers (1723–1796) worked for the Swedish East India Company (he was born in Sweden to Scottish parents) and spent time in Guangzhou, where he viewed buildings and gardens. The books which he subsequently published, *Designs of Chinese Buildings* (1757) and *A Dissertation on Oriental Gardening* (1772), were immensely influential throughout Europe, including Russia, and contributed greatly to the 18th-century European enthusiasm for chinoiserie. *Designs of Chinese Buildings* includes a section on "the Art of Laying Out Gardens among the Chinese," in which Chambers refers to his own experiences and also

Fig. 193   *Portrait of Tan Chet-Qua* (1770/1771)
J. H. Mortimer (1740–1779)
Oil on canvas
Royal College of Surgeons of England

This painting was originally described as a portrait of "a Chinese mandarin" but recent research

strongly suggests it represents Tan Chet-Qua. Tan's portrait also appears, a short distance behind William Chambers, in the celebrated group portrait of members of the Royal Academy 1771–2 by Johan Zoffany (1733–1810).

to information obtained from someone he calls Lepqua, otherwise unidentified (perhaps someone with the surname Nie, rendered in Cantonese pronunciation). The second edition of the *Dissertation on Oriental Gardening* (1773) includes "An Explanatory Discourse, by Tan Chet-Qua, of Quang-Chew-Fu, Gent." Although this "discourse" was almost if not entirely Chambers' own work, it is quite possible that he added to his knowledge of Chinese gardens through his acquaintance with Tan Chet-Qua (whose original Chinese name is unknown), a ceramic portrait artist from Guangdong who worked in London from 1769 to 1772 and was one of the earliest Chinese visitors to Britain (fig. 193). Together with *A Particular Account of the Emperor of China's Gardens near Pekin* [Beijing] (published in French in 1743 and in English translation in 1752) by the French missionary Jean-Denis Attiret (1702–1768), and illustrations of the imperial gardens sent back to Europe by Matteo Ripa (see Chapter Nine), Chambers' works influenced the new style of English landscape garden which transformed the grounds of aristocratic country houses in many European countries as well as estates in North America.

Botanical Illustration

European plant collectors who visited China in the 18th and early 19th centuries often employed Chinese artisan painters to illustrate the plants which they had "discovered." Before the invention of the glazed Wardian case in the 1830s, it was very difficult to transport live specimens on long sea voyages, and seeds might fail to germinate, so good-quality illustrations were often the best way to transmit knowledge of new species of plants. These Chinese artists, based in Guangzhou, were often highly skilled, but their names are almost unknown. The English botanist John Bradby Blake (1745–1773), who worked in Guangzhou for the British East India Company, did a great deal in his short life to promote knowledge and use of Chinese plants in the West. He worked closely with Chinese illustrators, especially one called Mai Xiu (Mak Sau in Cantonese), whose name he recorded as Mauk-Sow-U. Their beautifully detailed colored illustrations were much admired and often copied (fig. 194). In the early 1770s Blake was also responsible for bringing to Britain a young man, Huang Edong (written at the time as Whang-y-Tong and with various other spellings; c. 1753–after 1784), who had apparently been inspired by Tan Chet-Qua's successful visit. Huang's arrival as another early Chinese visitor was such a sensation that his portrait was painted in 1776 by the celebrity portraitist Sir Joshua Reynolds (fig. 195). Huang had impressed Blake with his knowledge of the cultivation and uses of plants and, speaking good English, he also worked with Blake as a translator. Thus we can see that, even though their names are far less well known than those of the European botanists, many people in China contributed to the exchange of botanical and horticultural knowledge between China and the West.

Fig. 194   Painting of white camellia, created by Bradby Blake with Mai Xiu (between 1770 and 1774)
Oak Spring Garden Foundation, Upperville, Virginia

Camellias of various colors and types had been cultivated in China as ornamental garden plants since at least the 8th century, but first became known to Europeans in the late 17th century, though only through monochrome engravings, written descriptions, and dried specimens. Mai Xiu and Bradby Blake's image, with its careful details of leaf and seed-capsule, was one of the earliest accurate colored depictions to reach Europe, and was frequently copied. Twenty years after Bradby Blake's death, the camellia had been established as a valued garden plant in Europe.

Fig. 195   *Portrait of Wang-Y-Tong* (1776)

Joshua Reynolds (1723–1792)
National Trust, Knole Park

As the portrait subject, Huang Edong looks slightly embarrassed by the very obviously orientalist chinoiserie elements which the artist has introduced, especially the display of his silk breeches and leggings.

APPENDICES

SUGGESTIONS FOR FURTHER READING

This is not a complete bibliography, just a guide to get you started and to indicate where some of the information in this book has come from. I have restricted it to (mostly) short pieces, in English, which are easily accessible, or at least accessible through a public or university library.

GENERAL

Chen Congzhou, *On Chinese Gardens [Shuo Yuan]*, tr. Mao Xinyi et al., Shanghai: Tongji University Press, 1984; New York: Better Link Press, 2008.

Chen Jianxing, *Gardens of Suzhou*, Beijing: China Travel Press, 2000 [excellent photos].

Fung, Stanislaus, "Guide to secondary sources on Chinese gardens", *Studies in the History of Gardens and Designed Landscapes*, 18:3, 1998, pp. 269–286.

Hardie, Alison, and Duncan M. Campbell, eds., *The Dumbarton Oaks Anthology of Chinese Garden Literature*, Washington, DC: Dumbarton Oaks, 2020 [a wide range of Chinese texts on gardens, in English translation].

Hu Dongchu, *The Way of the Virtuous: the Influence of Art and Philosophy on Chinese Garden Design*, Beijing: New World Press, 1991.

Keswick, Maggie, *The Chinese Garden: History, Art, and Architecture*, 3rd edition, London: Frances Lincoln, 2003.

Mowry, Robert D., "Chinese Scholars' Rocks: An Overview", *Worlds Within Worlds: The Richard Rosenblum Collection of Chinese Scholars' Rocks*, Cambridge, MA: Harvard University Art Museums, 1997, pp. 19–36. A very brief but useful introduction to "Chinese Gardens and Collectors' Rocks" is available at: https://www.metmuseum.org/toah/hd/cgrk/hd_cgrk.htm

Silbergeld, Jerome, "Beyond Suzhou: Region and Memory in the Gardens of Sichuan", *The Art Bulletin* 86 (2), June 2004, pp. 207–227 [not just about Sichuan but a useful summary of Chinese garden development].

Wang, Joseph Cho, *The Chinese Garden*, New York: Oxford University Press, 1998 [a concise introduction to the subject].

CHAPTER ONE

Schafer, Edward H., "Hunting Parks and Animal Enclosures in Ancient China", *Journal of the Economic and Social History of the Orient* 11.3 (October 1968), pp. 318–343.

Second Henan Field Team, Institute of Archaeology, CASS, "Palatial Garden Pond at the Shang City in Yanshi, Henan", *Chinese Archaeology*, vol. 7, no. 1, 2007, pp. 23–31; Du Jinpeng, "Palatial Garden Pond of the Early Shang", *Chinese Archaeology* vol. 7, no. 1, 2007, pp. 113–118.

Sima Xiang-ru, "Rhapsody on the Supreme Forest", in Burton Watson, tr., *Chinese Rhymeprose: Poems in the Fu Form from the Han and Six Dynasties*, New York, Columbia University Press, 1971, pp. 37–48.

Wu Liang shrines: https://barbierilow.faculty.history.ucsb.edu/Research/WuzhaishanRemastered/index.htm

CHAPTER TWO

Boynton, Grace M., "Notes on the Origin of Chinese Private Gardens", condensed from the Chinese of Wu Shih Ch'ang, *China Journal*, 23 (July 1935), pp. 17–22.

Ledderose, Lothar, "The Earthly Paradise: Religious Elements in Chinese Landscape Art", in Susan Bush & Christian Murck, eds., *Theories of the Arts in China*, Princeton, NJ: Princeton University Press, 1983, pp. 165–183.

Swartz, Wendy, "There's No Place Like Home: Xie Lingyun's Representation of His Estate in 'Rhapsody on Dwelling in the Mountains'", *Early Medieval China*, vol. 21, 2015, pp. 21–37.

Wilhelm, Hellmut, "Shih Ch'ung 石崇 and his Chin-ku-yüan 金谷園", *Monumenta Serica*, vol. 18, 1959, pp. 314–327.

Yang Xiaoshan, *Metamorphosis of the Private Sphere:*

Gardens and Objects in Tang-Song Poetry, Cambridge MA: Harvard University Asia Center, 2003.

CHAPTER THREE

Hargett, James M., "The Pleasure Parks of Kaifeng and Lin'an during the Sung (960–1279)", *Chinese Culture*, vol. 30, no.1, March 1989, pp. 61–78.

Hargett, James M., "Huizong's Magic Marchmount: The Genyue Pleasure Park of Kaifeng", *Monumenta Serica*, vol. 38, 1988–1989, pp. 1–48.

Harrist, Robert E., Jr, "Site Names and Their Meanings in the Garden of Solitary Enjoyment", *The Journal of Garden History*, vol. 13, no. 4, 1993, pp. 199–212.

Lee Hui-shu, *Exquisite Moments: West Lake and Southern Song Art*, New York: China Institute Gallery, 2001.

Makeham, John, "The Confucian role of names in traditional Chinese gardens", *Studies in the History of Gardens and Designed Landscapes*, 18:3, 1998, pp. 187–210.

Walton, Linda A., "Southern Sung Academies and the Construction of Sacred Space", in Wen-hsin Yeh, ed., *Landscape, Culture, and Power in Chinese Society*, Berkeley, CA: Institute of East Asian Studies, UC Berkeley, 1998, pp. 23–51.

West, Stephen H., "Spectacle, Ritual, and Social Relations: The Son of Heaven, Citizens, and Created Space in Imperial Gardens in the Northern Song", in Michel Conan, ed., *The Social Reception of Baroque Gardens*, Washington, DC: Dumbarton Oaks, 2004.

Wu Xin, "Yuelu Academy: Landscape and gardens of neo-Confucian pedagogy", *Studies in the History of Gardens and Designed Landscapes*, 25:3, 2005, pp. 156–190.

Xu Yinong, "Interplay of image and fact: the Pavilion of Surging Waves, Suzhou", *Studies in the History of Gardens and Designed Landscapes*, 19:3–4, 1999, pp. 288–301.

CHAPTER FOUR

Mote, Frederick W., "Confucian Eremitism in the Yüan Period", in Arthur F. Wright, ed., *Confucianism and Chinese Civilization*, Stanford, CA: Stanford University Press, 1964, pp. 252–290.

Steinhardt, Nancy Shatzman, "The Plan of Khubilai Khan's Imperial City", *Artibus Asiae*, vol. 44, no. 2/3, 1983, pp. 137–158.

Ye Tian and Hai Fang, "Research on the Historic Appearance of the Lion Grove from the Yuan Dynasty to the Republic of China", *Studies in the History of Gardens and Designed Landscapes*, 37:1, 2017, pp. 1–14 [note: "Zen hub" should be "Zen hut" throughout].

Vinograd, Richard, "Family Properties: Personal Context and Cultural Pattern in Wang Meng's 'Pien [Bian] Mountains' of 1366", *Ars Orientalis*, vol. 13, 1982, pp. 1–29.

Walton, Linda A., "Academy Landscapes and the Ritualization of Cultural Memory in China under the Mongols", in Michel Conan, ed., *Performance and Appropriation: Profane Rituals in Gardens and Landscapes*, Washington DC: Dumbarton Oaks, 2007, pp. 153–170.

CHAPTER FIVE

Clunas, Craig, *Fruitful Sites: Garden Culture in Ming Dynasty China*, London: Reaktion Books, 1996.

Hammond, Kenneth J., "Wang Shizhen's Yan Shan Garden essays: narrating a literati landscape", *Studies in the History of Gardens and Designed Landscapes*, 19:3–4, 1999, pp. 276–287.

Handlin Smith, Joanna F., "Gardens in Ch'i Piao-chia's [Qi Biaojia's] Social World: Wealth and Values in Late-Ming Kiangnan [Jiangnan]", *Journal of Asian Studies*, vol. 51, no. 1, February 1992, pp. 58–81.

Hu, Philip K., "The Shao Garden of Mi Wanzhong (1570–1628): revisiting a late Ming landscape through visual and literary sources", *Studies in the History of Gardens and Designed Landscapes*, 19:3–4, 1999, pp. 314–342.

Li, June, and James Cahill, *Paintings of Zhi Garden by Zhang Hong: Revisiting a Seventeenth-Century Chinese Garden*, Los Angeles, CA: Los Angeles County Museum of Art, 1996.

Stuart, Jan, "Ming dynasty gardens reconstructed in words and images", *Journal of Garden History*, vol.10, no. 3, 1990, pp. 162–172.

Wen Zhenheng, *The Elegant Life of the Chinese Literati: From the Chinese Classic, Treatise on Superfluous Things*, tr. Tony Blishen, Shanghai: Better Link Press, 2019, Chapter One: Studios and Retreats; Chapter Two: Flowers and Trees; Chapter Three: Water and Rocks.

CHAPTER SIX

Clunas, Craig, "Ideal and reality in the Ming garden", in L. Tjon Sie Fat & E. de Jong, eds., *The Authentic Garden: A Symposium on Gardens*, Leiden: The Clusius Foundation, 1991, pp. 197–205.

Clunas, Craig, *Screen of Kings: Royal Art and Power in Ming China*, London: Reaktion Books, 2013, Chapter 2: "The Kingly Landscape". [Note: Clunas uses "King" as the equivalent of the Chinese *wang*; I have used "Prince", more widely used in English for these imperial clan members in the late imperial period.]

CHAPTER SEVEN

Gao, Lei, & Jan Woudstra, "Repairing Broken Continuity: Garden Heritage in the Historic Villages Xidi and Hongcun, China", *Historic Environment*, vol. 23, no. 1, 2011, pp. 48–55.

Hardie, Alison, "Think Globally, Build Locally: Syncretism and Symbolism in the Garden of Sitting in Reclusion", *Studies in the History of Gardens and Designed Landscapes*, 26:4, 2006, pp. 295–308.

Hardie, Alison, "Washing the *wutong* tree: garden culture as an expression of women's gentility in the late Ming", in Daria Berg & Chloë Starr, eds., *The Quest for Gentility in China: Negotiations beyond gender and class*, London: Routledge, 2007, pp. 45–57.

Lee, Sylvia W. S., "'Co-branding' a *Cainü* and a Garden: How the Zhao Family Established Identities for Wen Shu (1595–1634) and Their Garden Residence Hanshan", *Nan Nü* 18.1, 2016, pp. 49–83.

CHAPTER EIGHT

Hardie, Alison, "The Life of a Seventeenth-Century Chinese Garden Designer: *The Biography of Zhang Nanyuan*, by Wu Weiye (1609–71)", *Garden History* 32/1, Spring 2004, pp. 137–140.

Hardie, Alison, "The Practical Side of Paradise: Garden Making in Ming Dynasty China", in Michael G. Lee and Kenneth I. Helphand, eds., *Technology and the Garden*, Washington DC: Dumbarton Oaks, 2014, pp. 155–167.

Ji Cheng, *The Craft of Gardens: The Classic Chinese Text on Garden Design*, tr. Alison Hardie, Shanghai: Better Link Press, 2012.

Métailié, Georges, *Science and Civilisation in China, Volume 6: Biology and Biological Technology, Part 4: Traditional Botany: An Ethnobotanical Approach*, Cambridge: Cambridge University Press, 2015 (chapter on horticultural techniques).

CHAPTER NINE

Berliner, Nancy Zeng, ed., *Juanqinzhai in the Qianlong Garden*, London: Scala Publishers Ltd., 2008.

Chen, K. S., & George N. Kates, "Prince Kung's Palace and Its Adjoining Garden in Peking", *Monumenta Serica*, vol. 5, 1940, pp. 1–80.

Cheng Liyao, *Royal Gardens: Private Gardens of the Imperial Family*, Jericho, NY: CN Times Books, 2015.

Forêt, Philippe, "The intended perception of the Imperial Gardens of Chengde in 1780", *Studies in the History of Gardens and Designed Landscapes*, 19:3–4, 1999, pp. 343–363.

Forêt, Philippe, *Mapping Chengde: The Qing Landscape Enterprise*, Honolulu: University of Hawai'i Press, 2000.

Holdsworth, May, *The Palace of Established Happiness: Restoring a Garden in the Forbidden City*, Beijing: Forbidden City Publishing House, 2008.

Siu, Victoria M., *Gardens of a Chinese Emperor: Imperial Creations of the Qianlong Era, 1736–1796*, Lanham, MD: Rowman & Littlefield, 2013.

Strassberg, Richard E., and Stephen H. Whiteman, *Thirty-Six Views: The Kangxi Emperor's Mountain Estate in Poetry and Prints*, Washington, DC: Dumbarton Oaks, 2016.

Rinaldi, Bianca Maria, *Ideas of Chinese Gardens: Western Accounts, 1300–1860*, Philadelphia, PA: University of Pennsylvania Press, 2016.

Whiteman, Steven H., *Where Dragon Veins Meet: The Kangxi Emperor and His Estate at Rehe*, Seattle, WA: University of Washington Press, 2020.

Wong, Young-tsu, *A Paradise Lost: The Imperial Garden Yuanming Yuan*, Honolulu: University of Hawai'i Press, 2001, Chapter 5: "Structure and Function".

CHAPTER TEN

Chung, Anita, *Drawing Boundaries: Architectural Images in Qing China*, Honolulu: University of Hawai'i Press, 2004, Chapter 5: "Moving Gardens: Yangzhou Representations I".

Meng Yue, "Re-envisioning the Great Interior: Gardens and the Upper Class between the Imperial and the 'Modern'", *Modern Chinese Literature and Culture*, vol. 14, no. 1, Spring 2002, pp. 1–49 [on merchant gardens of Yangzhou and Shanghai].

Meyer-Fong, Tobie, *Building Culture in Early Qing Yangzhou*, Stanford: Stanford University Press, 2003, Chapter 5: "The Triumph of Spectacle".

Richard, Josépha, "Uncovering the Garden of the Richest Man on Earth in Nineteenth-Century Canton: Howqua's Garden in Honam, China", *Garden History*, vol. 43, no. 2, 2015, pp. 168–181.

Zhang Yichi, "From Enclosure to Necessity: The Functions of Public Parks in the International Settlement of Shanghai, 1842–1943", *Garden History*, vol. 46, no. 2, 2018, pp. 170–183.

Zhang Yichi, "From 'Arcadia of the literati' to 'extravagant enclosure': the Tianjin salt merchant gardens of the Qing Dynasty", *Landscape Research*, 45:7, 2020, pp. 789–801.

CHAPTER ELEVEN

Curtis's Botanical Magazine (Royal Botanic Gardens, Kew), vol. 34, no. 4, December 2017, special issue on John Bradby Blake.

Li Yu, extracts from *Random Ventures in Idleness*, tr. Duncan M. Campbell, in Alison Hardie and Duncan M. Campbell eds., *The Dumbarton Oaks Anthology of Chinese Garden Literature*, Washington, DC: Dumbarton Oaks, 2020, pp. 537–545.

Richard, Josépha, "Collecting Chinese Flora: Eighteenth- to Nineteenth-Century Sino-British Scientific and Cultural Exchanges as Seen through British Collections of China Trade Paintings", *Ming Qing Yanjiu*, 24, 2020, pp. 209–244.

van Hecken, J. L., and W. A. Grootaers, "The Half-Acre Garden, Pan-Mou Yüan [Banmu yuan]: A Manchu Residence in Peking", *Monumenta Serica*, vol. 18, 1959, pp. 360–387.

NOTES

1 *The Book of Songs*, tr. Arthur Waley, London: George Allen & Unwin, 1937, p. 35.

2 *"Zhao Hun (The Summons of the Soul)"*, tr. David Hawkes, *Ch'u Tz'u [Chuci]: The Songs of the South*, Oxford: Clarendon Press, 1959, pp. 105, 106.

3 Sima Qian, *The Grand Scribe's Records [Shiji]*, tr. William H. Nienhauser, Jr, Bloomington & Indianapolis: Indiana University Press, 1994, 1.15.

4 Hellmut Wilhelm, "Shih Ch'ung [Shi Chong] and his Chin-ku-yüan [Jingu yuan]", *Monumenta Serica* 18 (1959), p. 326.

5 Translation by W. J. F. Jenner in *Memories of Loyang: Yang Hsüan-chih and the Lost Capital (493–534)*, Oxford: Clarendon Press, 1981, p. 207.

6 Translation by G. W. Robinson in *Poems of Wang Wei*, Harmondsworth: Penguin Books, 1973, p. 28. There is an enormous number of translations attempting to convey the full meaning of this expressive but cryptic poem.

7 Translation by Xiaoshan Yang in Hardie and Campbell eds., *The Dumbarton Oaks Anthology of Chinese Garden Literature*, Washington, DC: Dumbarton Oaks, 2020, p. 131.

8 Quotation from "Lyric to the tune *Huan xi sha*," tr. Eugene Eoyang, in Hardie and Campbell eds., *The Dumbarton Oaks Anthology of Chinese Garden Literature*, p. 232.

9 The other three artists were Ni Zan, Huang Gongwang, and Wu Zhen.

10 Shen Fu, *Six Records of a Floating Life*, tr. Leonard Pratt & Chiang Su-hui, Harmondsworth: Penguin Books, 1983, p. 136.

11 Linda Walton, "Academy Landscapes and the Ritualization of Cultural Memory in China under the Mongols," in Michel Conan ed., *Performance and Appropriation: Profane Rituals in Gardens and Landscapes*, Washington DC: Dumbarton Oaks, 2007, p. 160.

12 Walton, "Academy Landscapes," p. 161.

13 From Xie Zhaozhe (1567–1624), *Wuzazu*, tr. Alison Hardie, *Chinese Garden Pleasures: An Appreciation*, Shanghai: Better Link Press, 2014, p. 29.

14 Zhang Dai (1597–c. 1684), letter to Qi Biaojia, tr. Duncan M. Campbell, in Hardie and Campbell eds., *The Dumbarton Oaks Anthology of Chinese Garden Literature*, p. 435.

15 Translation from the Ming *Veritable Records* in Craig Clunas, *Empire of Great Brightness: Visual and Material Cultures of Ming China*, London: Reaktion Books, 2007, p. 140.

16 Galeote Pereira, "Certain Reports of China," in C. R. Boxer, *South China in the Sixteenth Century*, Bangkok: Orchid Press, 2004, p. 42. The English translation was made by Richard Willis in 1577 from an Italian version published in 1565.

17 Translated in Craig Clunas, *Screen of Kings: Royal Art and Power in Ming China*, London: Reaktion Books, 2013, p. 38.

18 Craig Clunas, "Ideal and reality in the Ming garden," *The Authentic Garden: A Symposium on Gardens*, ed. L. Tjon Sie Fat & E. de Jong, Leiden: The Clusius Foundation, 1991, p. 197.

19 *The Plum in the Golden Vase or, Chin P'ing Mei, Volume Two: The Rivals*, tr. David Tod Roy, Princeton: Princeton University Press, 2013.

20 Sylvia W. S. Lee, "'Co-branding' a *Cainü* and a Garden: How the Zhao Family Established Identities for Wen Shu (1595–1634) and Their Garden Residence Hanshan," *Nan Nü* 18.1 (2016), p. 66.

21 Chen Suoyun, "The Biography of Mountain Man Zhang, the Recliner on Rocks," tr. Alison Hardie, in Hardie and Campbell eds., *The Dumbarton Oaks Anthology of Chinese Garden Literature*, pp. 473–474.

22 Wen Zhenheng, tr. Tony Blishen, *The Elegant Life of the Chinese Literati: from the Chinese Classic, Treatise on Superfluous Things*, Shanghai: Better Link Press, 2019, p. 31.

23 Translation by Duncan M. Campbell in *The Dumbarton Oaks Anthology of Chinese Garden Literature*, p. 171.

24 Jonathan D. Spence, *Emperor of China: Portrait of K'ang-hsi [Kangxi]*, Harmondsworth: Penguin Books, 1974, p. 7.

25 Spence, *Emperor of China*, p. 8.

26 Translation from Zhang Dai, "Lu Yungu zhuan"(*Langhuan wenji, juan* 4), by Gu Kai, "'Painting-like' and 'Lifelike': Two Ideas in Artificial Mountain Making in Ye Xie's 'On Artificial Mountains'", *Studies in the History of Gardens & Designed Landscapes*, 41:3, 2021, pp. 225–233.

27 Wu Hung, "Beyond Stereotypes: The Twelve Beauties in Qing Court Art and 'The Dream of the Red Chamber'", in Ellen Widmer and Kang-i Sun Chang eds., *Writing Women in Late Imperial China*, Stanford, CA: Stanford University Press, 1997, p. 324.

28 Wu, "Beyond Stereotypes", pp. 327–328.

29 Daria Berg, *Women and the Literary World in Early Modern China, 1580–1700*, London: Routledge, 2013, pp. 225, 229.

30 Translation by Duncan M. Campbell in *The Dumbarton Oaks Anthology of Chinese Garden Literature*, p. 590.

DATES OF THE CHINESE DYNASTIES

Xia Dynasty（夏）..2070–1600 BC
Shang Dynasty（商）..1600–1046 BC
Zhou Dynasty（周）..1046–256 BC
    Western Zhou Dynasty（西周）..................................1046–771 BC
    Eastern Zhou Dynasty（东周）..................................770–256 BC
        Spring and Autumn Period（春秋）......................770–476 BC
        Warring States Period（战国）............................475–221 BC
Qin Dynasty（秦）..221–206 BC
Han Dynasty（汉）..206 BC–AD 220
    Western Han Dynasty（西汉）....................................206 BC–AD 25
    Eastern Han Dynasty（东汉）....................................25–220
Three Kingdoms（三国）..220–280
    Wei（魏）..220–265
    Shu Han（蜀）..221–263
    Wu（吴）..222–280
Jin Dynasty（晋）..265–420
    Western Jin Dynasty（西晋）......................................265–316
    Eastern Jin Dynasty（东晋）......................................317–420
Northern and Southern Dynasties（南北朝）......................420–589
    Southern Dynasties（南朝）..420–589
    Liang Dynasty（梁）..502–557
    Northern Dynasties（北朝）..439–581
Sui Dynasty（隋）..581–618
Tang Dynasty（唐）..618–907
Five Dynasties and Ten Kingdoms（五代十国）..................907–960
    Five Dynasties（五代）..907–960
    Ten Kingdoms（十国）..902–979
Song Dynasty（宋）..960–1279
    Northern Song Dynasty（北宋）..................................960–1127
    Southern Song Dynasty（南宋）..................................1127–1279
Liao Dynasty（辽）..916–1125
Jin Dynasty（金）..1115–1234
Xixia Dynasty (or Tangut)（西夏）......................................1038–1227
Yuan Dynasty（元）..1279–1368
Ming Dynasty（明）..1368–1644
Qing Dynasty（清）..1644–1911

INDEX